NINE MORE CLINICAL CASES

NINE MORE CLINICAL CASES

Case Studies in Clinical Pastoral Care, Counseling and Psychotherapy

RAYMOND J. LAWRENCE

CPSP
press

An extensive critical review of the clinical pastoral cases published in: *Case Studies in Spiritual Care: Healthcare Chaplaincy Assessments, Interventions & Outcomes*, George Fitchett, and Steve Nolan, Eds., London: Jessica Kingsley Publishers, 2018.

©2020 Raymond J. Lawrence

9 8 7 6 5 4 3 2 1

CPSP Press
P.O. Box 162
Times Square Station
New York, NY 10108
CPSPPress.org

Publisher's Cataloging-in-Publication data:

Names: Lawrence, Raymond J., author.

Title: Nine more clinical cases : case studies in clinical pastoral care , counseling , and psychotherapy / Raymond J. Lawrence.

Description: Includes bibliographical references. | New York, NY: CPSP Press, 2020.

Identifiers: ISBN 978-0-578-73334-0

Subjects: LCSH Psychotherapy--Case studies. | Pastoral counseling--Case studies. | Pastoral care--Case studies. | Caring--Religious aspects--Christianity--Case studies. | BISAC RELIGION / Christian Ministry / Counseling & Recovery | PSYCHOLOGY / Psychotherapy / Counseling

Classification: LCC BV4012.2 .L29 2020 | DDC 259--dc23

Cover image: Lauren Kay Jin Kuo
Model: Thorin Schriber
Design: Krista Argiropolis / Verbum Icon

For Armen D. Jorjorian

1919-1973

who made me a pastoral psychotherapist.

CONTENTS

FOREWORD

Lest some of those new to the discussion think that Raymond Lawrence writes critiques only of books written by George Fitchett and Steve Nolan, this being his second, let it be noted that he has served as a thoughtful critic of clinical pastoral chaplaincy since the late 1990s.

He puts his critiques in writing and invites others to critique his own thoughts. Lawrence pays attention to criticism, his own and others', toward trying to build an improved clinical pastoral chaplaincy. Let me cite but two examples of Lawrence's comments written years before Fitchett and Nolan published their first book. He writes, *Our continuing vitality [as chaplains] will be determined by our ability to nurture a receptiveness to criticism.... And elsewhere, We will have to be resolute and diligent if we want to nurture a capacity for the self-critical in our midst....* In this present volume Lawrence asserts, *Criticism is the lifeblood of the clinical pastoral movement.* That is, Lawrence views serious critique as a means to strengthen clinical pastoral work.

Decade by decade, he has conveyed his increasing appreciation of the wisdom discovered and disseminated by the de facto founder of professional chaplaincy starting in the mid-1920s, Anton Theophilus Boisen. Boisen encouraged patients, practitioners, and organizations alike to be frank about their shortcomings and failures. In 1927 he wrote, *It is ever the task of the church to disturb the consciences of [people] in regard to the quality of the life they are living in order that they may turn before it is too late and be made whole.*

Lawrence keeps cycling back to a key question: "What is the clinical pastoral chaplain's real job?" He is quite clear, that praying with the patient as a *pro forma* act is not an essential part of the work. He views prayer as important primarily in regard to how it might help both chaplain and patient better to understand what is on the patient's mind. *If a patient or client of a pastoral psychotherapist would requested prayer, a competent pastoral psychotherapist would ask the patient what he or she wished to pray about. In that way, by the time the patient explained, the prayer would already be essentially done – which, of course, is the point.*

Boisen discussed it similarly: *I do believe in prayer. I believe that its chief function is ... to find out what is wanted ... and to enable us to draw upon sources of strength which will make it possible for us to accomplish our task....* Thus prayer in clinical pastoral chaplaincy as psychotherapy is not something done automatically – often as the chaplain is on the way out the door. Prayer, if the patient requests it, can become an important part of the serious mutual effort to understand the nature of the patient's suffering. The job of the pastoral psychotherapist, working as one in the tradition of Freud, is to *listen* and *make connections* if at all possible. This listening and making connections takes time and effort but it is at the heart of clinical pastoral chaplaincy and psychotherapy as a caring process.

In working with those who are suffering, bewildered, or vulnerable, Lawrence, after Boisen, encourages us to take a patient's every thought quite seriously, even while examining it closely in terms of its potential validity. As Boisen phrased it, the task is to *begin with ...[the patient's] experiences and learn to see through his [or her] eyes...* According to Boisen, *The effectiveness of the therapist will ... depend upon [the therapist's] capacity ... to think with [the patient] about his [or her] real problems and to kindle ... faith in a better self which can be realized.*

This attempt at mutual understanding – what Boisen called, *"cooperative inquiry"* – is not an "academic" or "labeling" exercise. It is, rather, an attempt at grasping and then addressing the patient's unique needs. He viewed this *working with* a patient – in essence a psychotherapy – as helping both parties to become better over time at living life. Boisen spoke of this as, *the conscious, systematic, cooperative effort to test the ... suggested solutions of a difficulty or perplexity by means of empirical observation and experimentation in order to arrive at the universal relationships or laws, which may be involved.* Such cooperative inquiry takes time, but every minute spent in *listening* – and in *making connections* – Lawrence emphasizes, reaps valuable benefits. A frequent criticism that he voices throughout this book is that the chaplain is talking too much and listening too little.

In conclusion, let me suggest that one go back and read – or re-read – *Nine Clinical Cases,* Lawrence's critique of Fitchett and Nolan's first book. I also recommend that one take a look at anything and everything written by Anton Theophilus Boisen and about his clinical work.

Robert Charles Powell, MD, PhD

PREFACE

This monograph is a response to the second in a series of collections of case studies compiled by George Fitchett and Steve Nolan and is also the second published critique by me, printed herein. My critiques have been, of course, uninvited. As the reader will note, there is a wide philosophical gap between the theoretical and practical positions represented in the Fitchett-Nolan monograph and my position. Let the reader decide which is more representative of the authentic clinical pastoral training movement. Let the reader decide which position is more therapeutic. Let the reader determine what posture most accurately speaks for Anton Boisen, the founder of the clinical pastoral training movement. And let the reader decide whether some new direction should be called for at large. But no one is beyond the reach of criticism. Criticism is the lifeblood of the clinical pastoral training movement.

I applaud Fitchett and Nolan for initiating this process. It is quite strange that the clinical pastoral training movement, which began in the 1920s with Anton Boisen's examination of clinical cases, has, in more recent times, altogether avoided serious examination of clinical work. Today, almost a century after Boisen's revolutionary work, one can find very few published clinical cases illustrating and critiquing the work of pastoral clinicians. Much academic theory has been published, but very little case material. I believe we all learn much more from cases than from theoretical discourse. Thus I believe Fitchett and Nolan have begun, or revived, a valuable approach to clinical pastoral work and especially to the training aspect of that work, and I roundly applaud them for that. I hope they consider my critical responses, though quite sharp, to be equally valuable, and entirely in the spirit of the clinical pastoral training movement founded by Anton Boisen.

INTRODUCTION

When Anton Boisen launched the clinical pastoral movement in 1925, his purpose was to train his fellow ministers to take up the role of pastoral psychotherapists, which Boisen believed was their inheritance. Understanding the human psyche and understanding mental disturbance, and how to treat it, was Boisen's laser focus. He claimed to have been immediately enlightened by his reading Freud while in psychiatric lock-up. On release, he set out to train ministers to follow the Freudian approach in counseling troubled people. But so far as is known, Boisen never had any psychoanalytic psychotherapy himself. (Of course, neither did Freud!)

Boisen's trainees in his first training group in 1925 were not explicitly training to be clinical chaplains. They did not even present themselves to patients as religious workers. They were officially paid orderlies who gathered stories of the patients' lives and met later in the day in a group to discuss the patients whom they had conversed with during their chores. The question they carried within their interface with patients was: What is the nature of the suffering of these people? And how might we function therapeutically concerning them? Boisen never thought that saying a prayer over a patient would effect a cure. Nor did he credit advice-giving. His declaration (slightly rephrased by me) was, "It's not what the minister says to the patient, but what the patient says to the minister." Freud had set him forth on his professional journey.

Boisen concluded that listening to patients long enough and making connections in their stories would likely reveal the source of their suffering and open the door to healing. Boisen trained his students (they were all seminary students at the time) to become pastoral psychotherapists. Boisen himself famously said that there was nothing Freud could do that a clinically trained minister could not do. And Freud himself, though there is no evidence that he knew of Boisen, would undoubtedly have agreed as he made clear in his 1926 book, *The Question of Lay Analysis*.

Boisen's approach to the training of seminarians, and later ministers, and even laypeople, to do psychotherapy evolved through the decades to become what would have been unrecognizable to Boisen himself.

The impetus of this transformation was persistent anxiety among pastors about their role. The anxiety stemmed from several sources. In the beginning, Richard Cabot, MD was Boisen's champion. He taught him the case method at Harvard. And he even went so far as to finance him. Boisen had no money. Without Cabot's moral and financial support, Boisen, a just-released psychiatric patient, may not have achieved anything. With Cabot's strong support, Boisen was within two years made Director of Chaplains at Worcester State Hospital, an amazing elevation from that of the involuntary psychiatric patient to psychiatric hospital department head in two years, in 1924.

But the relationship between the two men soon floundered. By 1930 they were no longer colleagues but passionate adversaries. Cabot had long-held psychiatry in contempt. Boisen, on the other hand, studied Freud and saw that his approach was the only credible route to healing. (He was understandably not so impressed with Jung or Adler.) This divergence of the two founding fathers of clinical pastoral training, Boisen and Cabot, shaped all the subsequent history of the clinical pastoral movement. With Boisen, the chaplains were functional psychotherapists, though, of course, assiduously avoiding the nomenclature. With Cabot, the chaplain's principal function was to pray. Through the course of the twentieth century, this dialectic prevailed and was fiercely argued by many.

There were inhibiting factors that reigned among pastoral psychotherapists, and chief among them was language use. Chaplains were prone to defuse the language and to refer to themselves as counselors rather than psychotherapists. They elected to avoid the developing struggle with psychiatry in the marketplace; this was a tragic pulling of their punch on the part of the pastors. But in truth, they likely had little choice in the mercantile world of hospitals where the physician is king, and the psychiatrist is first a physician.

Chaplains generally reduced their professional potency by calling themselves counselors, a much less potent but more politically acceptable label. Furthermore, the prayer warriors, heirs of Cabot, increasingly exerted their influence. For most people, prayer became a much simpler and more easily understood function for a chaplain. "He came to pray," they liked to say. Or a nurse might say, "Chaplain, go say a little prayer for Mrs. Jones in 219. She's upset." It is also more comfortable for a chaplain to say that he or she "came to pray" than to say that he or she came "to listen and decipher whether there was a need here for someone to talk to about suffering or problems." And if there is that need, the chaplain is available. And thus, for many, the role of chaplaincy slipped into the primary function of a prayer warrior. To be sure, not all clinical chaplains took that route. By mid-century, a significant majority of mainline Protestant ministers in the U.S. were directly or indirectly followers of Boisen and conceived of their role as that of the pastoral psychotherapist.

Another unspoken appeal of prayer as the primary function of the chaplain is that prayer provides a handy tool for exiting a patient's room. When visiting a patient, there is always some degree of anxiety about how and when to leave. It's awkward to say goodbye. Chaplains sought an easy exit, a simple way to close the visit, especially since they are not on the fifty-minute clock. A straightforward approach is to offer a summary of the visit. But that requires serious thought. A one-size-fits-all parting prayer is much less work. Then one can make a respectable exit.

Thus it is noteworthy that in Fitchett's and Nolan's second collection of case studies (under review here), almost every patient visit ends with a prayer. We know, of course, why pastors do that. It not only makes for a smooth exit, but it also ensures that the pastors can feel like something legitimate has been accomplished in the visit. For a chaplain to play the role of a listening and therapeutic presence, absent religious rituals, is not satisfactory to the more insecure. However, the comfort of prayer, if it is of comfort, dilutes the essential function of the chaplain in Boisen's construct. In the latter's construct, the function of listening and, if possible, making connections makes such chaplains true heirs of Freud.

In 1965, a critical split occurred in the clinical pastoral movement in the United States. The American Association of Pastoral Counselors (AAPC) was formed, and many of those ministers who held to the Boisen-Freud approach to patient work split off from the wider Boisen community, leaving the line chaplains to their own devices. It was an innovation vehemently opposed by the influential Seward Hiltner, who objected to pastoral psychotherapy becoming separated from congregational life.

But it was a tad more convoluted than that. After 1930, the original Boisen organization, the Council for the Clinical Training of Theological Students (CCTTS), had itself split into four groups of competing philosophies, each outwardly professing to follow Boisen, at least to some extent. In each of the groups, with the notable exception of the Southern Baptists, who were deeply Freudian, there was an increasing hesitancy to attach the label of psychotherapy to their work. At the same time, there was an impulse among many, especially those who followed the leadership of Boisen's chief rival, Dr. Richard Cabot, to emphasize the need for chaplains to pray with patients. To pray or not to pray became, if somewhat soto voce, the dominant theme in the continuing internecine conflict.

Those who joined the new AAPC saw themselves generally as disciples of Boisen and Freud, though few of them were willing to say so boldly. They commonly understood their work as involving psychotherapy, but publicly they usually labeled it "pastoral counseling." That strategy, in effect, gave away all the specifically psychotherapeutic field to physicians and was a notable professional retreat. Had the founders possessed real professional authority, they would have labeled their new community AAPP, the American Association of Pastoral Psychotherapists. Once again, religious leadership pulled its punch, and as regards the prayer issue, rarely, if ever, did an AAPC-certified counselor pray with a patient. To do so would be seen as a blurring of roles with a counseling or psychotherapeutic client or patient. It would be considered an inappropriate insertion of religious ideology into a psychotherapeutic course.

Boisen did not think clinical pastoral training was very promising when established in general hospitals. Such hospitals did not provide enough time to work with patients, who tended to have short stays, and it was difficult, as well, for a chaplain to carve out uninterrupted time with patients. Physicians in general hospitals rarely give way when it comes to chaplains' time with patients. The medical doctor is king in a general hospital. In a psychiatric hospital, the chaplain's time with patients is respected and protected by physicians. Chaplains do not flit around praying with patients in the way they often do in general hospitals. Here chaplains are generally seen as fellow psychotherapists.

There exists a gulf today between those pastors who view themselves as prayer warriors (an accurate though somewhat pejorative label) and those who view themselves as pastoral psychotherapists. This gulf has been embodied in the three-decade organizational divide between the College of

Pastoral Supervision and Psychotherapy (CPSP) and the Association for Clinical Pastoral Education (ACPE), with its sibling, the American Association of Pastoral Counselors (AAPC). The latter two organizations have entirely abandoned the Boisen philosophy of pastoral work. They have also recently merged.

If a patient or client of a pastoral psychotherapist requested prayer, a competent pastoral psychotherapist would ask the patient what he or she wished to pray about. In that way, by the time the patient explained, the prayer would already be essentially done—which, of course, is the point. Why should a therapist pray for a patient? The typical patient is fully capable of praying for him/herself. And that, of course, is the focus of psychotherapy. The pastoral psychotherapist has no exclusive line to God, nor does he or she ever know what the content or the longings of the heart of a patient might be, until such a time as they are disclosed.

***

Most of the cases examined below refer to spiritual care rather than pastoral care; this is a flawed attempt to avoid any appearance of promoting anything Christian. But it is also a failure to recognize the universality of the role and symbol of pastor or shepherd that permeates every culture and religion. With remarkable candor, Steve Nolan confesses that the words spiritual and spirituality have yet to be defined in the culture at large. What he means is that the words have been washed through history and have both gained and lost certain connotations. We know what the words used to mean, but current usage has radically shifted the connotations of the category, and not for the better.

I suspect that spiritual will not be clearly defined in the broader culture in our lifetimes. In ancient times spiritual connoted a life force, centered in the breath or breathing, as in a spirited horse, an earthy category. Today spiritual seems to imply something up there, out there. The concept of spirituality has no feet on the ground. Such thinking does not unite people. It separates them. Pastoral is a much more appropriate concept for chaplains – or anyone – because it implies care for one another, a non-negotiable act. If we do not care for each other, then all the community is lost. Pastoral is not hostage to Christianity. It is used by other religions, especially Judaism and Islam. Pastoral is not even hostage to religion itself. The atheist Sigmund Freud referred to himself as "a secular pastoral worker." He meant that he cared for and nurtured his clients and friends. That posture is the best religion there is, with or without theism.

A "Viewpoint" article in the *Journal of the American Medical Association* (August 8, 2017, Vol. 318, No. 6) called for a more explicit focus on spirituality among clinicians, stating that spirituality is often considered outside the realm of science. It is indeed outside the realm of science; it is bereft of definition. However, pastoral does have definition and can be examined clinically.

The one valuable contribution that a clinical chaplain can provide for people of any religion or no religion is competent psychotherapy or, if one prefers to take a more self-effacing posture, psychoanalytically-oriented pastoral counseling. It should involve no initiative whatsoever on the part of the chaplain to pray or to interject any specific form of religion. Getting all the wildly various religions together in one place to pray is never going to happen, at least not in this world. The attributes of the different deities will never permit it. And why would we need such a gathering anyway? We can do more for each other relating pastorally, simply as one human being to another, and leave organizational religion at the door. Human beings struggle over relationships. They struggle over the complexity of integrating the forces of the unconscious with their particular consciousness. And they struggle over simply living together in the world without slaughtering one another. A clinical chaplain without any specific religious agenda can be a blessing to such suffering people everywhere.

***

On the matter of prayer, most institutional chaplains today refer to a god who is a kind of one-size-fits-all deity. Their prayers are on the order of "to whom it may concern." This posture satisfies no one. In Judaism and Islam, God is a jealous God, tolerating no rivals, but discrete religions promote rivals. Hinduism postulates multiple gods: Shiva, Brahma, Vishnu, the monkey god, and all the rest. Buddhism is, on the other hand, generally atheistic. There is the eternal Buddha, but there are no gods. Christianity proclaims monotheism with one breath and a triune God of Father, Son, and Holy Ghost the next. And some Christians worship the Virgin Mary, making it at least four. Others worship a whole bevy of saints. When an innocent chaplain wanders into prayer, whether aware or not, he or she enters a hornet's nest of competing interests. But by melding all these gods into one benign entity overall, a Great Benefactor in the Sky, they offend everyone. Hardly anyone will say that out loud, however.

People who are serious practitioners of a particular religion are generally uninterested in a bowdlerized god. Who wants to read a bowdlerized Shakespeare? The bowdlerizing of religion was relatively easy fifty years ago when Catholic, Protestant, and Jew was the extent of religious practice in most Western countries, and the Hebrew Bible the glue that held them together. Still, that state of affairs no longer holds. The National Conference of Christians and Jews (NCCJ), which held sway in the mid-twentieth century, has gone out of business or, to be more accurate, it has reconfigured itself as the National Conference of Community and Justice. It is no longer about religion but has diverted into ethics—not a bad diversion.

Prayer in the United States at this time in our history has become something on the order of a state religion. But it is a religion with no ethics and little other content beyond a vague nationalism. Congress regularly appoints a chaplain, and members of Congress stage what they call "Prayer Breakfasts," where a religion without substance is hyped. What the prayer lobby has done has been to generate a one-size-fits-all god for public occasions. Prayers are addressed, more or less, "to whom it may concern," to a bowdlerized god who is of little substance and attracts even less interest. Wouldn't silence be preferred? Since God is silent, can we not do the same? The Quakers learned that lesson several centuries ago. Silence is much to be preferred over the bland pronouncements of the typical hospital chaplain, trying to speak to the center of the universe while avoiding any offense to Yahweh, Buddha, Jesus, the Virgin Mary, and all the saints, Allah, Shiva and all the many additional gods of Hinduism. A constant theme with the chaplains of both monographs by Fitchett and Nolan is the urgency to pray over patients.

Clinical pastoral work should be wed to no religion at all. Least of all, should it be wed to Christianity. It is no wonder that the clinical pastoral movement has not moved much beyond imperial Christianity. Too many of its practitioners are now evangelists in disguise. Clinical pastoral practitioners must respect and defer to all religions for what they are, but commit to none. Clinicians should see the value in each religion, but also stand critical of each for whatever dehumanizing tendencies it may have. And they should sup with any cultural form of religion with a very long spoon.

A RIFF ON THE COVER

The first signal of what these cases promote is displayed on the cover of the book, *Case Studies in Spiritual Care*, where the chaplain, with both hands, is holding, apparently, a female patient's hand, while sitting cheek by jowl with her. Of course, there are times when it is appropriate for a clinical chaplain or pastor to hold a patient's hand or to sit that close and face-to-face. However, the elevation of handholding intimacy in this way on the cover of this monograph plays to the current weakness in chaplain functioning. I refer to over-functioning. It's a dog whistle to those who prefer to get close, touch, give advice and direction to patients, and to pray.

From a clinical perspective, this is treatment without diagnosis. Additionally, such a portrait could not exist in the current environment featuring a male chaplain. A male chaplain presented in that close, intimate physicality with a woman—or possibly even another man—would call down fire from the gods of the politically correct along with the multitude of androphobes. The editors solve that problem by portraying two women in such a position.

Such close handholding could be viewed as the culmination of a long and significant relationship, and even a variation on the ancient Christian kiss of peace. Each is the culmination of something, a meaningful relationship, or even life itself— a benediction of sorts. Both handholding and the kiss of peace represent a kind of coda that rounds out and concludes a meaningful experience. But such intimacy is never described in the book for which it provides a cover. In any case, such intimacy would unlikely be appropriate very early in a pastoral relationship. And general-hospital chaplains rarely have the kind of extended time with patients that permit such intimacy to develop.

To make matters worse, many chaplains today view the handholding and the immediate intimacy as the thing itself rather than the culmination of something, the summary of a developed relationship. But handholding cannot be seen as the thing itself without cheapening the significance of the pastoral relationship.

The thing itself, namely clinical pastoral care and counseling— the cure of souls— requires a kind of hospitable distance for the most part. The chaplain or minister who comes too close, too soon, and becomes too entangled in the life, the body, and the experiences of the patient or parishioner, is rendered impotent by this loss of distance and clinical objectivity.

Thus pastors are rarely if ever able to become a therapeutic presence to members of their own family. They are, of course, by the nature of things too entangled already, by necessity, with family members. (Nor does a wise physician attempt to treat friends or members of his or her own family.) A therapeutic presence, with its mandatory distance and its objective eye, is impossible to establish within the context of an already complex and significant relationship.

The cover on this monograph thus signals what it for the most part contains: an anxious chaplaincy, too eager to dissolve the boundaries between people, but of course, only if both parties are female.

Thus this monograph sends unfortunate signals before one ever opens the book.

CASE 1

THAT'S GREAT!
YOU CAN TELL US HOW
YOU ARE FEELING

By Chaplains Liz Bryson, Paul and Sally Nash,
serving at Birmingham (England) Children's Hospital.

Mark, a recently and severely physically disabled 11-year-old boy with a brain tumor

While three chaplains are named as authors in this case, the only data presented in addition to the background is the data of two visits by Chaplain Bryson, reported to have been "some months" apart. Chaplain Bryson's visits seem to be the only recorded interaction between patient and chaplains. It is reported that Chaplain Bryson made many other visits to the patient, and perhaps the other two chaplains visited as well, but data on those visits, if they occurred, are not reported.

Bryson is a volunteer chaplain with a postgraduate certificate in pediatric chaplaincy from the Institute for Children, Youth, and Mission at Staffordshire University. It seems that the Institute is under the provenance of the University even though mission and university do not sound compatible to my ear.

The voice, in this case, seems to be entirely that of Bryson, listed as the first among the three authors. Bryson describes the details of her visits with Mark. Among other disabilities, Mark was unable to talk or write or, it seems, even to stand; he also had limited use of his hands. The chaplain brought to the bedside clay, pebbles, dolls, and other instruments for play. The chaplain engaged Mark in a variety of play activities. She spoke with

1

him, or rather she talked to him and for him, or attempted to, and the reported non-verbal indications were that Mark much appreciated her presence, kindness, and attention. Given his condition and the extensiveness of his limitations, that is indeed credible. Who else would have the courage and stamina to attempt to communicate with a pre-teen who cannot speak? I suppose that only a mother could do that. Bryson is a mother, and she herself had a child, now deceased, who suffered a brain tumor and died two years before her undertaking chaplaincy work with similar children. So we can assume that she knows the territory. She also has other children.

The chaplain could tell when Mark was pleased or happy, but she could not tell much, if anything, about what he was thinking.

People such as these chaplains, who are willing to give attention to such disabled children, must surely be admired by us all. And anyone must be grateful to Chaplain Bryson for giving her time and energy to Mark, especially since the only specific feedback he could give her is non-verbal. Mark eventually lived until age twenty-seven. No one could believe that Mark had anything resembling a rewarding life.

Chaplain Bryson contends that she sets out to identify whether a patient's need is religious, spiritual, or pastoral. The reader is left in the dark as to how she defines the three categories. No data is presented as to how she distinguishes these three areas of professional focus. But since spiritual has already appropriately been declared by the co-editor, Steve Nolan, as undefined, one wonders how she could assess an undefined category. The other two needs that she attempts to address are religious and pastoral and are reasonably easy to define. A religious need is commonly assumed to be a need related to functioning in the context of a particular religion, for example, an individual's need for a sacrament. In such a case, the normal process would be to attempt to requisition a representative of that religion who might follow up with a visit. A pastoral need has an entirely different connotation. Such a need does not impinge on any specific religion at all. It connotes a generic need for care and protection, such as a shepherd might provide for his or her sheep. Even atheists can have pastoral needs, as Sigmund Freud contended.

The chaplain, and I would also presume the chaplaincy team, is accustomed to using the term "spiritual play" to describe its functioning with the children-patients who cannot communicate verbally. This spiritual play is said to develop around the concept and objective of "seeking an interpretive spiritual encounter" or ISE. But how can one define an ISE if the notion of spiritual itself remains inchoate? The team supports this theoretical posture by citing its own published writings, of which I am ignorant. However, ISE seems to me an inflated self-serving concept that serves no real purpose, as it is unhooked from anything definable, as if spiritual has been granted definitional immunity.

In Bryson's first reported and described a pastoral visit to Mark, the chaplain brought beads for making such things as bracelets. The chaplain explained to Mark that the proposed activity they were about to engage in was "spiritual care beading." This explanation was certainly as understandable to the brain-damaged Mark as a description of Sheldon Kopp's *Eschatological Laundry List* might have been. What could "spiritual care beading" have possibly have meant to a normal eleven-year-old boy, much less one with a seriously impaired brain function? In fact, what could it likely mean to a person of any age? Beading is beading. What makes spiritual care beading different from just beading? It sounds as if the chaplain's urgency is to authenticate her activity and gives her work some significant-sounding meaning. But would it not be enough simply to invest time with Mark, lay aside any need to put a religious label on it, and lay aside any need to hype the commendable human service here? The chaplain's time with Mark, and her demonstrated interest in him, is blessed enough and needs no phony religious whipped-cream topping.

Furthermore, Bryson writes, "the spiritual care beading activity enabled me to communicate respect and dignity and to seek to build self-worth and value ... through Mark's obvious choice of colored beads, I was able to identify the need for love, security, hope, establishing identity, self-worth, and value, and a sense of belonging, acceptance, and connectedness." Bryson is beginning to sound like someone smoking dope. Must we then presume that she means red is for love and white is for hope, or did we get that backward? I suppose this is what George Fitchett means when he touts evidence-based outcomes.

Of course, as we might anticipate, Mark was described by the chaplain as pleased and enthusiastic. Given his dreadful predicament, I suspect Mark was pleased and enthusiastic over any serious attention or investment of time on his behalf by any kind person. And I do not doubt whatsoever that the chaplain here was kindly. But I do believe she is poorly trained and seduced by those who tempt her to claim too much and to do so in flowery language. What she did with Mark needs no gloss.

Finally, the chaplain felt the need to reassure Mark of how much he was securely loved by his "mum and dad and by God," and how much he belonged to his family and the hospital community. However, saying such nice things does not make them so. Such words take on the character of Shakespeare's "Methinks the lady doth protest too much." In other words, the chaplain put herself under suspicion for mouthing such high-sounding claims about how vital Mark was to his family, friends, and the hospital community. Even an eleven-year-old with brain damage may be suspicious of such glittering claims. More likely, though we have no data on this, Mark's family was heartbroken over Mark's condition and prognosis, perhaps even at their wit's end. It may well be that Mark felt—irrationally—some responsibility for this grim scenario. But that line of thinking does not emerge. Without a family interview and a very significant time investment, I see no possibility of exploring such an issue with Mark.

As the chaplain began to leave after the first recorded visit, Mark's father observed, referring to the spiritual care beads, "You've really enjoyed that Mark, haven't you?" Mark nodded. The chaplain departed, reassuring the family of her prayers. (I wonder who might monitor these promises of prayer.) The chaplain concluded that Mark was more relaxed than when she arrived, which is certainly credible.

In the second visit, "some months later," the chaplain reports that Mark was feeling very frustrated with his physical limitations, undoubtedly rooted in his continuing inability to communicate verbally or in writing, not to mention his lack of mobility. She generously shared with Mark some pebbles she collected on the north Cornish coast. She and Mark created stick figures for a paste-on. She then opened an envelope with stickers portraying sad and happy feelings. Mark responded positively to this exercise. With his weak left hand, he pasted on both happy and sad figures. Indeed, he was likely full of sorrow. Perhaps he was pleased to get any attention at all. I wonder how many chaplains have the courage to visit an eleven-year-old who is unable to communicate verbally.

PUBLISHED CRITICAL RESPONSE BY HANS EVERS

Evers, a pediatric chaplain himself, mostly summarizes what the chaplain has accomplished. He does assert that "the direct contact with the patient has transcendent meaning" and that the chaplain is "in but not of the world." My reply to that is that clinicians have no data from any other worlds, if there are any, nor do clinicians as clinicians know anything about "transcendent meaning." Evers must decide whether he ever wants to be a clinician.

PUBLISHED CRITICAL RESPONSE BY JENNIFER BAIRD

Baird offers a discourse on the pediatric chaplain's role, which is not what I would call a critical response.

MY CRITICAL RESPONSE

This case is heartbreaking. Although I am critical of the summary conclusions of the chaplains, I must say that my admiration extends to Chaplain Bryson for the gifts of her time and energy to this afflicted young boy who has now gone on to his reward. Yes, it is a heartbreaking case.

I could find no mention in this case of religious identification, or lack thereof. That qualifies as missing clinical data. The absence makes the chaplain's promise to pray for the family a bit incongruous. Was the family a family of non-believers? Perhaps. If so, the promise of prayer would be even more inappropriate.

When the chaplain declares that Mark "had a deep awareness of his inner being and a sense of transcendence that needed nurturing and supporting," she has again attempted a bridge too far. How could she possibly know that a boy who was unable to talk or write was experiencing such profound thoughts? By her description, Mark could communicate only by nodding, shaking his head, or using his unsteady left hand. The chaplain is no longer a clinician examining the body. She has transformed into a fantasist.

In her assessment section the chaplain claims that through Mark's clear choice of colored beads, she was able to identify his "need for love, security, hope, establishing identity, self-worth, and value, and a sense of belonging, acceptance, and connectedness." I get it. She's smoking that dope again. Of course a psychiatrist would file it under "projections."

The chaplain continues: "I had a sense of a real lift in his spirit during and after an encounter." That is a credible observation. But I would conjecture that Mark was simply happy, perhaps, to have anyone visit him and to attempt to communicate with him. But then the chaplain follows up with Vygotsky's concept of the "zone of proximal development," a theory that suggests that the need for problem solving in children can be achievable only with the support and encouragement of another person. I confess not to have read Vygotsky. Still, if he has written something seeking to demonstrate that children need the support and encouragement of another to solve problems, I have to think he belabors the obvious with pretentious theories.

The chaplain reports that the spiritual practice of Ignatius was used to encourage Mark in his awareness of the transcendent. The chaplain here ventures out onto thin ice. Perhaps the family is somehow connected to Roman Catholicism, but if so, I missed it. I believe an attempt to introduce any child-patient to any form of religious practice is beyond the bounds of a clinician's role and quite hazardous professionally and politically, whether or not the patient happens to be Catholic. And the fact that the child is not able to communicate verbally makes it even more inappropriate.

Regarding the outcomes of the chaplain's work, Bryson judged that she and Mark connected and found the presence of the transcendent—"the wounded healer himself"—to be there in the midst of the encounter. She judged that Mark "was able to build a relationship with God, the transcendent other." I suppose Chaplain Bryson feels confident in asserting that because Mark is unable to speak and refute her.

Finally, she concluded that the encounter with Mark "was in part measured by the way that our evidence-based spiritual care principles have been incorporated into practice." But what evidence is she referring to? She claims to have seen profound spiritual insight and development in Mark's journey. But she files this claim by title, without a shred of clinical data to support it. She concludes, "The involvement and faithfulness of a transcendent and very personal God in the human journey is an enduring reason for hope." This final claim is patently fake. She certainly cannot have any clinical evidence of the workings of a God. Nor any clinical evidence that there is a god. The summary conclusions, in this case, demonstrate a stunning un-clinical exercise in imagination.

In the multi-faith world in which we find ourselves, the promotion of any one religious ideology invites well-deserved and severe criticism, indeed even hostility. God, if there are gods, does not submit to a clinical review. Clinical chaplains are mandated first to remain clinical.

This loving care of Mark cannot be denied. But the efforts to crowbar into the pastoral relationship various high-sounding religious categories is not only unwarranted, but it is also quite embarrassing.

I must also register what is a relatively minor, but I think an essential, irritant in this case, and that is the reference throughout to Mark's mother as "Mum." *Case Studies in Spiritual Care* purports to be a serious scholarly document. Why not refer to Mark's mother as just that? Or is the chaplain also going to use "Papa" or "Daddy" for the father? It appears to me to be special pleading for recognition of intimacy with the family. But Chaplain Bryson is allegedly a professional clinical chaplain. Such cute lingo communicating ultra-familiarity diminishes the chaplain in the serious clinical world where human health and life are on the line. (Some might claim that "mum" is an accepted professional term in Great Britain. If so, I stand corrected.)

In summary, the chaplains in this case may very well have been a blessing to this afflicted and undoubtedly lonely young boy. The fact that Chaplain Bryson spent any time with him at all is commendable, though it is not clear how much time she did spend. Only three visits are noted. That Bryson and the medical team wanted him to feel loved is admirable and commendable, to say the very least. But I wish that Bryson could have laid aside the need to inflate the caring work that she certainly accomplished with glittering, phony, "spiritual" exaggerations. She did not need them!

CASE 2
"SHE'S ALREADY
DONE SO MUCH"

By Chaplain Patrick Jinks

Sarah, diagnosed prenatally with Trisomy 18, and her family

Jinks, who is certified by the Association of Professional Chaplains in the U.S. and a (U.S.) Presbyterian Church minister, presents the case of Sarah, diagnosed with Trisomy 18, meaning she suffers a very serious genetic defect. Her fate is that she will not fully develop in the womb, and will not likely live very long even if she is born alive. Fewer than ten percent of such babies live as long as a year. They suffer intensive and costly medical treatment, and the word "suffer" is used advisedly. The doctors in this instance proposed termination of the pregnancy, but the parents refused. The parents "put their faith in God's healing intervention." The chaplain supported that, deferring to their allegedly strong Pentecostal Christian faith. They believed that God had given them this pregnancy, and that was that. Thus, even before the child was born, a host of ethical concerns was broached.

The first bump in the road in this clinical case was the determination by the parents to make medical decisions based on faith, however that faith might be defined. The chaplain writes that their deep-seated, faith-informed desire and hope for baby Sarah to be born alive should be supported. My view is that what is labeled faith should be appropriately labeled a rejection of the physicians' best prognosis and an expectation of exceptional results founded on magical thinking. Serious religious people have never defined faith as embracing magical thinking. They would classify jumping out of a high-flying airplane without a parachute and hoping to live through the experience because one was inspired by God as magical thinking, not faith. But the chaplain here was persuaded by what he viewed as the parents' "strong faith." It would have been more accurate to conclude that the parents rejected the physicians' prognosis in favor of an expectation of a magical intervention by a god. It would be interesting to know what the financial terms of this decision involved. We presume that the public paid the bill, which was surely gargantuan.

Since the parents declared themselves Pentecostals, the chaplain inquired as to their openness for prayer. The wisdom of that move is dubious. A typical Presbyterian minister is not likely to connect readily with a Pentecostal in prayer. Worse still, an offer of prayer, on any basis, would seem to nurture the parents' already worrisome religious irrationality regarding the medical problem and the prognosis. A clinical chaplain's role certainly should not entail the buttressing of any religious constructs he or she encounters. The clinical role should look more like agnosticism about any religious ideology and, more particularly, the ideology that cavalierly and irrationally trumps informed medical judgment.

In a C-section delivery, Sarah was, though premature, born alive, thus defying the odds. The parents took this as a sign from God that he would provide for Sarah. More prayers followed, offering thanksgiving for the safe delivery. The parents were renewed in their hope that Sarah would eventually go home with them. As could have been expected, they were wrong.

The parents were then fearful that the medical team would decline to resuscitate Sarah if she became debilitated. The parents also had a three-year-old son to care for. In the chaplain's first visit, he had inquired about the mother's openness for prayer, and of course, being Pentecostal, she readily acceded to the offer, even from a Presbyterian. In this act, the chaplain reinforced the mother's irrationality.

At four months, Sarah, still confined to neo-natal ICU, had not left the hospital. The physicians were not in agreement on a plan of treatment. Meanwhile, the husband was on the road all week for work. The other child, a three-year-old, was being neglected. The mother asked the chaplain, "What do we do about our son?" as if his welfare was not considered at the outset of this venture. Generous efforts were made by staff to ease family stress.

At five months, Sarah was transferred to a heart center in another city for the repair of her heart defect, putting further stress on the family and especially the neglected three-year-old. Following heart surgery, it was not possible to wean Sarah from mechanical respiratory support. She was given a tracheostomy to help her breathe. The family concluded that she was a gift of God because she had survived nearly six months in defiance of the medical prognosis. While she had not become a six-month-old developmentally, she did interact to some extent with people. Then she rapidly declined and died. It seems that there had been little or no support from their church. There was no record provided for any visit from her home church, even though it was said that the mother was very active there. The mother said to the chaplain, "You were Sarah's pastor."

Chaplain Jinks did a spiritual assessment of the patient modeled after his own five-point framework of "Love, Faith, Hope, Virtue, and Beauty." (He neglected to include "Pie in the Sky.") He concluded that Sarah's spiritual need was to be held and bonded with love. But has there ever been a patient for whom that is not the case? He argued that they all had experienced the joy and beauty of a new life. It seems that Chaplain Jinks is prone to impose, like Pollyanna, a positive spin on things. From my perspective, I fail to see much joy and beauty in an afflicted infant who barely makes contact with other beings, is never able to leave her crib, and spends her last month struggling to breathe with mechanical support. No one reports on the pain level of the infant because she, of course, is unable to communicate beyond crying. I would evaluate that as a brief and tortured life.

But the parents concluded that Sarah had a significant and worthy quality of life, that she was a child with disabilities who experienced relationship, love, and affection. I would not want to be reincarnated as a child in that family.

In conclusion, Chaplain Jinks says that using a program of age-specific spiritual needs, he offered play, song, prayer, reading, and presence as tangible interventions to facilitate Sarah's experience of the sacred and holy. He claims to have helped Sarah experience joy and happiness and to encounter the holy by way of her family's faith tradition. Chaplain Jinks has at best documented that he has a rich fantasy life.

PUBLISHED CRITICAL RESPONSE BY HANS EVERS

Evers contends that Jinks embodied assurance of the presence of God and that his contact with the family "had transcendent meaning." These two claims may or may not be accurate, but certainly, neither is a *clinical* judgment. Evers further asserts that though chaplains claim a place within the hospital organization and as members of hospital teams, they are "in but not of the world." However, clinical, by definition, specifically attends only to this world. Perhaps Evers is called to be a spiritual chaplain, not a clinical chaplain.

PUBLISHED CRITICAL RESPONSE BY JENNIFER BAIRD

Baird asserts that Chaplain Jinks here used prayer to help communicate an understanding of the mother's concerns and that this was a smart therapeutic strategy. I think it not smart at all, but a trivial misuse of prayer and misleading of the mother.

MY CRITICAL RESPONSE

As I have suggested already, the chaplain here is quite a Pollyanna. For starters, we have a dreadfully afflicted infant, diagnosed *in utero* as so afflicted and destined for such a short and challenging life that some of the physicians advised abortion. But for reasons not clear, the parents were adamant that they would carry the child to term. The birth was premature, and the infant, named Sarah, never left in-patient hospital care, nor even her bed. She was responsive to contact with others, but barely, and short of six months she was dead. Would they repeat the same over again? No one answers that question, but the implied answer is yes. I find even the implication of such an answer unfathomable. There are some conditions worse than death. There are some conditions under which being born is surely no blessing at all.

The chaplain waxes on about the joy and beauty of a new life and about how Sarah successfully reached significant milestones. I have to think he is disassociating here. The report suggests that the chaplain saw her only five times. Thus he was not likely forced to contemplate on a daily basis her dreadful condition and grim fate. I find nothing beautiful about a newborn who is destined to remain in her crib for six months, face major surgery, breathe through a tracheostomy, and then die; this is not a tale of joy for anyone—parents, medical personnel, or observers. It is grievous for all concerned. Why should any compassionate person wish that on any infant? It isn't as if everyone was blindsided and did their best. All were warned of the likely outcome when the child was *in utero*. The warning turned out to be accurate.

CASE 3
"HE IS DISAPPOINTED
I AM NOT THE SON HE WANTED.
I TRIED AND TRIED
TO DENY I AM A GIRL."

By Chaplain Janet Hanson

Vicki, a male-to-female transgender veteran

Chaplain Janet Hanson presents pseudonymous "Vicki," a case of a troubled male-to-female transgender military veteran. Hanson elaborates "distal stress" and "proximal stress," which are simply her unnecessarily esoteric words to communicate negative experiences from others as well as internalized conflicts. Vicki was dismissed from the military because of drinking problems. She has a history of difficulty with her Catholic family, as one might expect.

Chaplain Hanson is a chaplain at the Veterans Administration Hospital where Vicki is a patient. She is an ordained United Methodist minister, a certified Clinical Pastoral Educator with the Association for Clinical Pastoral Education, and a member of the LGBT community in which she holds a leadership position.

Hanson reports that her "spiritual care" for Vicki consisted of one fifty-minute visit. She began with, "Tell me how I can support you today?" Hanson's first words have already put her in a box. "Support" is an extremely limiting description of the proper work of a pastoral clinician. But Hanson kept her promise. Support was all she attempted.

Hanson professes to use a programmatic approach referred to as Acceptance and Commitment Therapy (ACT).

Vicki explained that she has been talking to her therapist, and relating that her family and her church have rejected her. She tried being a boy and doing boy things with her father, but she "sucked at it." Her feminine impulses "only came back stronger, like a weed." Her father, she said, finally gave up on her. While she did not say so, she was also rejected by her prior therapists, who gave up on her as well, and thus referred her to Hanson.

Hanson objected to her use of the word "weed" and recommended a more positive metaphor, suggesting she delight in who she is. Then both women launched into some vitriol about Catholic hypocrisy around sexual issues, settling on Jesus' love and acceptance as a contrast. Hanson then interjected a negative judgment of priests "who can't keep it in their pants." The dialogue began to sound like a war of women against men.

Then Vicki related a powerful spiritual experience she had with her dead mother, receiving the message that her mother loves her. This visionary experience seems to have been mediated through another troubled young woman. The chaplain accepted this report at face value.

Finally, the chaplain encouraged Vicki to try the Gay Pride parade coming up soon, and encouraged her also to get involved with churches that might be receptive of LGBT people.

Chaplain Hanson judged that the outcome of their session left Vicki feeling more blessed in God's eyes and that she better understood the struggle of the "coming out" process. Hanson also affirmed Vicki's experience of her communication with her dead mother via another marginalized person.

PUBLISHED CRITICAL RESPONSE BY ANDREW TODD

Todd begins by acknowledging that chaplains in the UK, where he resides, are not rooted in the clinical pastoral model. And indeed, it seems so; this case is a stark illustration of what they might be missing. What Todd does not know is that many American pastors who mouth clinical pastoral language are not rooted in that model either. There are lots of ways to miss a train. Todd adds that theological reflection is more an English concern. That might be commendable, depending on what is meant by theology. If they follow Paul Pruyser's assertion of what constitutes theological reflection, they are not far removed from the historic clinical pastoral approach, if at all. But I find no evidence of any reading of Pruyser.

Todd then, astutely I think, suggests that the ACT model tends to over-direct the chaplain's responses. Todd could have added, parenthetically, that this case appears to be a case of Behavior Modification Gone Wild.

Todd also notes, I think insightfully, that the metaphor "like a weed," used by Vicki, was evocative and begged exploration. The chaplain therapist's attempt to suppress it appears all the more ill-conceived.

PUBLISHED CRITICAL RESPONSE BY JAMES A. NIEUWSMA

Nieuwsma notes that this case and the subsequent one are both focused on sex, which for him brings up Freud. (I wish he had elaborated on that comment.) He also notices the introduction of the weed metaphor by Vicki and thinks that Chaplain Hanson is too cautious in declining to engage it. However, Nieuwsma knows Hanson personally, suggesting that the personal relationship pressured him into being too cautious in his critique of Hanson's approach.

MY CRITICAL RESPONSE

It seems unfortunate to me that the pastoral role, in this case, is relegated to the superficial, and that the real therapy is left to secular and possibly (or, should I say, likely) non-pastoral and or non-religious resources. This case dramatizes the general state of pastoral work today. Pastors often do the superficial, lightweight, fluff work, and leave the serious work to others. Vicki is sent by her therapist to the chaplain to receive "spiritual care." Thus the chaplain is painted in a corner as "not a therapist" and is prepared to offer something that has no definition - spiritual care. Anton Boisen must be rolling over in his grave.

The chaplain, in this case, leads off by asking how she can provide support, by implication limiting herself at the start. A patient may be contemplating taking some destructive action against herself or others, an action which would not call for support. The effective pastoral clinician is required first to *listen* rather than to *support*. Competent listening is indeed support, but the pastoral task does not end there; a competent pastoral clinician may also be called upon to query, prod, challenge, inform, or confront the one asking for help. The verb "support" is an inadequate summary description of the pastoral psychotherapeutic task.

The chaplain in this case can also be charged with not paying attention. "I sucked at it," Vicki says, about her inability or unwillingness to learn how to play baseball to please her father. Her use of language is striking here, as Nieuwsma, above, has pointed out. "Sucking" connotes predominantly an oral erotic action. Shouldn't we wonder what is being communicated here? The language has the marks of something else that Vicki wants to reveal or discuss, or more likely this is an unintended message from her unconscious. Either way, a competent counselor or therapist would be expected to pursue such seemingly off-the-wall language, such obscure messages. I had the immediate association that the counselee might have been signaling her wish to revert to a male homosexual role rather than the more radical one of a total of feminization. But that is merely my association, and in any case should be checked out with the counselee, himself or herself.

Next, the chaplain seems to want to put a positive spin on the supplicant's story. "You have accepted yourself and your gender: Is that right?" The question should be why the chaplain is here attempting to close off options when she is still in the first minutes of the counseling sessions

Then the chaplain suggests that the unacceptable sexual feelings would not go away. "Nope," says Vicki. "They only came back stronger, like a weed." The critic Nieuwsma, above, already pointed out the need for the counselor to attempt to unpack the weed metaphor. The chaplain, however, rejects this metaphor and suggests a more positive one. She seeks to silence or repress the struggling woman's metaphors rather than to explore them. This counseling session is more like a brainwashing or a fifty-minute course in public relations than an attempt at healing.

Give the chaplain therapist a D-minus.

CASE 4
"I WAS ABLE TO GO
TO CONFESSION."

By Valerie C. Sanders

Mrs. Helen, a survivor of military sexual trauma, perpetrated by a religious leader

Chaplain Sanders is an African Methodist Episcopal Church minister and staff chaplain with the Veterans Administration. She is a licensed marriage and family therapist with over twenty years of experience.

Mrs. Helen is described as a victim of military sexual trauma, referred to as MST. Statistics are cited that claim that 41% of women veterans have reported MST. Sanders argues that the numbers are skewed by under-reporting, and this would seem to assert – astonishingly –that the majority of women in the military have been sexually violated. Is this possible? Some authorities suggest that it is.

Mrs. Helen was a sixty-five-year-old veteran who had been lately overcome by memories of having been sexually violated by a Catholic priest while serving as a nurse in the military. Because of shame and guilt, she kept the story to herself for several decades. The alleged violator was a Catholic priest-chaplain who fondled her breasts as she slept seated next to him on a long military excursion by bus.

At an earlier time, Mrs. Helen had been raped by a fellow service member who had given her a ride home from some event, went into the house with her, and raped her there in her own home. She did not report the rape but rather continued a collegial relationship with the rapist, and within a year, she married him. Mrs. Helen shared that the rape had been difficult, but that she had gotten over it, whereas the molestation on the bus, the fondling of her breasts, had caused her more considerable emotional damage, which she had not gotten over. The chaplain therapist did not seem to notice that the patient has a recurring problem related to her sexuality.

The therapist in this case claims to have used ACT principles to work with Mrs. Helen. ACT purports "to transform unbearable pain into livable disappointment." ACT is characterized as encouraging clients to "hold and move, recalling pleasurable experiences." (ACT is attributed to Hayes and Lillis, 2012, which I have not researched.)

It is asserted that Mrs. Helen earlier underwent cognitive processing therapy (CPT), described as a specific type of cognitive-behavioral therapy often used to treat post-traumatic stress disorder. The therapy was provided in the MST clinic. She claimed not to have responded well to CPT because she felt challenged to identify what her role might have been in the molestation, and felt that she was being blamed inappropriately for the molestation.

Next, Mrs. Helen undertook therapy under the treatment of Sanders herself. The referral was informal. A psychologist reported that "maybe a chaplain could help." The psychologist communicated that she believed that Mrs. Helen was stuck due to some of her spiritual understandings.

Sanders undertook the treatment of Mrs. Helen, employing ACT, with the stated goal of "transforming unbearable pain into psychological flexibility."

In her first session with Chaplain Sanders, to which Sanders gives the title "Confiding her Story," Mrs. Helen shared that she knew all the priests at the military base. It seems that Mrs. Helen was something of "church mouse," as we used to say. She was a regular attendee at masses, and thus got to know all the priests in her orbit. The disturbing incident occurred on a military excursion, Mrs. Helen serendipitously found a seat on the bus next to a priest. It seems she boarded the bus late, and the seat next to the priest was the only one available. Mrs. Helen shared that she was a little bit excited to sit beside a priest during this extended journey. One has to be suspicious that she set herself up for that, knowing that most people might avoid seats next to a priest and thus would leave the last available seat next to him open. Into the journey, she reports that she fell asleep and was awakened to find the priest fondling her breasts. She was shocked, confused, and mortified, but kept the account entirely to herself for decades.

Session 2 is not reported by Chaplain Sanders. I wonder why not.

Session 3 is entitled by Chaplain Sanders "Present-Moment Awareness." The chaplain therapist attempted to help Mrs. Helen "observe her difficult feelings and memories of the past" and her anxieties about the future. The goal was to release the power and influence of her memories. The chaplain then introduced the benefits of meditation and mindfulness practices. Mrs. Helen countered by reminding the chaplain that she is a Catholic, and is not sure such practices are consistent with her faith. Seeming to be unhearing, the chaplain next proposed another mindfulness exercise, asking Mrs. Helen to close her eyes. Mrs. Helen inquired what the purpose of that exercise might be, adding that it had been challenging for her to stay focused. The chaplain explained what she was attempting to accomplish, offering a way for her to avoid becoming overwhelmed by her feelings.

It is noteworthy that the chaplain's discourse in the verbatim section occupies about sixty-two lines in this account, and Mrs. Helen's only seventeen. I suggest that this session be relabeled as "Sermonic Therapy." Alternatively, it might be labeled Freudian "talk therapy turned upside down," in which the therapist talks and the patient listens.

Session 4 is not described.

Session 5 is entitled "Defusion." The word defusion does not appear in my dictionary. *Defuse*, my consultants inform me, comes out of the military world, and means "to make less harmful," and its usage is increasingly common.

The chaplain concluded that Mrs. Helen was bound by the shame she had kept locked in her heart, along with the guilt that she carried with her for her feelings of anger toward her perpetrator. The chaplain introduced Mrs. Helen to the idea of "cognitive defusion." She invited her to "look at her thoughts, feelings, and memories, those barriers that cause you to feel stuck and prevent you ...from being able to confess your anger to a priest."

Mrs. Helen said, "I am ashamed that I was violated by a priest. I feel guilt and shame because I can't let go of the anger. I am embarrassed that, as a practicing Catholic, I have been unable to forgive him. I am afraid that no one would believe me. Why would anyone believe me over a priest?"

Next, the chaplain created a fantasy and invited Mrs. Helen to respond to it. The fantasy was that Mrs. Helen is driving a bus and that all those who abused her are passengers. They threaten Mrs. Helen. They come forward and crowd her in a threatening manner while she drives. She

19

then tells them that she will not steer in the right direction until they sit down. But they continue to threaten her. (Part of this account of the fantasy appears garbled in the published record.)

The chaplain then asked, "What are some of the things that the passengers are saying to you?"

Mrs. Helen responded, "God will never forgive you for your unforgiving heart."

The chaplain continued, "And the gang moves from the back of the bus to the front, directly behind you, and they have got louder."

Mrs. Helen replied, "I just feel overwhelmed by the gang of thoughts."

Another hundred plus words from the chaplain, and Mrs. Helen interjected: "They are always lurking and have been for forty years."

The chaplain asked, "What if these passengers could not hurt you or make you drive in a different direction? What if all they can do is come to the front of the bus and be scary?"

Mrs. Helen said, "Hmm."

Another speech by the chaplain, who concluded with, "it's really about shifting your focus to what matters most to you and being able to navigate your bus in the direction that you want it to go in."

In summary, once again, the chaplain has been talking considerably more than the patient.

Session 6 is labeled "Values Clarification." The chaplain introduced the "ACT Values Sort Cards," consisting of fifty cards, each identifying a value. She instructed Mrs. Helen to place each card in one of a stack of three categories: "not important," "somewhat important," and "very important." In the "very important" pile, there was love, because Christ died for each of us. She also placed in the "very important" pile her desire to find and confront her "perpetrator." She also put in the "very important" pile the wished-for receipt of an acknowledgment and an apology from the Catholic Church and the Archdiocese of the Military.

Session 7 is not disclosed.

Session 8 is called "Committed Action." In ACT, as Chaplain Sanders explains, committed action occurs when steps are taken that are guided and informed by values.

In this session, Mrs. Helen reported, "I did it! I was able to go to confession." She had found a young priest who performed the sacrament of confession as he sat in the church pews in the nave of his church. She confessed to him right there in the open.

"He was able to listen to me and was very apologetic for what happened to me at the hands of the priest. He was sincerely grieved by my story. In the end, he actually asked if he could hug me."

Her therapist responded, "He sounds very affirming of your pain."

But something remained missing for Mrs. Helen, according to the therapist. She had hoped the young priest would tell her how to release her anger, and he did not. So in the absence of a remedy, Mrs. Helen continued for another 15 weeks of ACT therapy. What she might have accomplished in the subsequent 15 weeks is not disclosed and is anyone's guess.

I wonder. Was Mrs. Helen hoping for more than that hug from the new young priest?

PUBLISHED CRITICAL RESPONSE BY ANDREW TODD

Todd rightly observes that the ACT approach seems to over-direct the chaplain's response.

In his section on Theological Reflection, Todd focuses entirely on the patients' relationships with the Catholic Church and its seemingly legalistic stance. While I concur with that judgment, I do not think that the patient's difficulty, in this case, is organizational. I doubt that changing her religious affiliation would be all that therapeutic. The seeming legalism of the Catholic Church, I think, connects with issues in Mrs. Helen's unconscious, or perhaps one feeds on the other. Both the Catholic Church and a great many non-Catholic churches do what they can to repress sexuality in both thought and deed. Mrs. Helen is just trying to be a good Christian and not having much fun with it.

PUBLISHED CRITICAL RESPONSE BY JASON A. NIEUWSMA

Nieuwsma points out that both this case and the previous one depict problems of sexuality, and that it is difficult to avoid recalling Freud. Yes, indeed; give Nieuwsma a box of Mars Bars. Unfortunately, he does not elaborate, but he discloses that he knows the chaplain in this case as well as the previous one. I take that to mean that he is reluctant to be seriously critical in this instance. He is wise on that score. Making an uninvited and penetrating critique of persons one knows in other contexts invites trouble.

Contrary to Todd, he argues that the ACT principles were effectively employed here, and concludes with the assertion that the chaplain therapist here was a powerful restorative force of spiritual authority, perhaps even of divine representation. That was probably what he had to say to an acquaintance who might know where to find him. In that claim, however, Nieuwsma moved out of the clinical and into the world of fantasy.

MY CRITICAL RESPONSE

It is not clear to me what the pastoral therapist was hoping to accomplish in this case. She did far too much talking. She also directed several exercises, the purpose of which was unclear to me, such as instructing Mrs. Helen to imagine that she is watching leaves float down a stream, observing phenomena floating by. It seems to me a silly exercise and might result in even more passivity. I conclude that this chaplain therapist holds the view that healing comes through strengthening the ego function to repress unconscious material more effectively. But Mrs. Helen's superego, if one follows the psychoanalytic construct, is already dictating her life and wearing her down. She seems already to have closeted away far too much stuff in her unconscious.

Mrs. Helen is focused obsessionally on sexual issues, but her focus is skewed and chock-full of denial. One might guess, for example, that her alleged rapist, whom she married, received a non-verbal message that she wanted sex but could not allow herself to ask for it, and thus *got herself* raped. The man must not have been a real rapist, because she married and lived with him subsequently. And one might guess that the priest on the bus received a covert message that he had sexually aroused her and thus followed up with fondling, a very human response. Finally, the priest who held his confessions in the nave of the church likely picked up some amount of sexual desire from Mrs. Helen, leading him to ask her for the hug. Even priests sometimes get turned on. This could suggest that Mrs. Helen has separated her ego from her sexual desires, and as a result is living a dangerously split existence. The chaplain therapist, in this case, seems oblivious to all this rather stark and troubling data. Thus this case shows the chaplain therapist to be oblivious of the reality of the unconscious and its power to communicate to others willy-nilly by way of non-verbal signals.

It seems clear that Mrs. Helen has introjected the Catholic teaching that sex is justified only by way of an intent to procreate, and she has made herself a prisoner to that teaching. Since she is of an age in which she is no longer able to procreate, perhaps she categorizes all sexual overtures as invasive and predatory, all the while desperately seeking them.

The critic Nieuwsma likely hits the nail on the head when he says that all this reminds him of Freud. This is the stuff of deep therapy. Can Mrs. Helen come to see herself as a woman desirous of sex, even perhaps desperately desirous, and as a woman who might be signaling her desires to others, however covertly. The therapist in this case seems oblivious to such possibilities.

The therapist here does not listen. In part she is impaired by the baggage of her ACT theory, the substance of which is such that it should be relabeled "Think About Something Else Therapy." We could call it TASET instead of ACT.

Thus it appears that Mrs. Helen is in dire need of psychotherapy, but not the sort of behavior modification offered by Chaplain Sanders. But whomever she elects to work with therapeutically, the prognosis cannot be promising. A person who for forty years has obsessed over a minor sexual episode of being fondled by a priest on a bus in the company of many other people, and who married her rapist, is apt to be highly resistant to a resolution of any sort of her conflicted relationship to sexual pleasure.

CASE 5
"GOD IS JUST TOO BUSY
FOR US RIGHT NOW"

By Jessica Bratt Carle

Paul, a 10-year-old white male, transitioning from a tertiary medical center to pediatric in-patient psychiatric care

NOTE: At this point in the monograph, the editors shifted the focus of cases to be critiqued to cases that demonstrated the work of the chaplain as ritual leader. Thus this moves somewhat away from the previous critiques, which focused on the clinical pastoral problem of the "body in bed" so to speak. (Clinical is derived from the Greek word klinē, meaning bed.) This reviewer will nevertheless remain focused on the clinical, disregarding the desired focus of the editors. As the reader can see, the cases are rich with clinical data.

Chaplain Carle describes herself as a white woman pastor of the Reformed Church in America in her late twenties at the time of this encounter. She is a graduate of Princeton Theological Seminary and did her clinical training at the National Institutes of Health in Bethesda and Yale-New Haven Hospital. She is certified by the Association of Professional Chaplains. At the time of this visit, she was serving a 1500-bed tertiary hospital.

Paul was a ten-year-old white male transitioning from a tertiary medical center to a pediatric in-patient psychiatric hospital. He engaged in self-harming behavior, such as banging his head against the wall.

The case began when the mother, whom the chart registered as bi-polar, called requesting that her son be baptized before being transferred to psychiatric care "within the next hour," also adding that she wanted to see a priest, presumably Catholic. The father is described as both absent and abusive.

The chaplain intended to explore the request for baptism. She introduced herself to the mother: "Hi, I'm Jessica. I'm a chaplain here at the hospital. I'm sorry if I woke you, but I did want to stop by, so I didn't miss you before you and Paul left. I heard you were hoping to speak to a chaplain before you left."

The mother replied that she was hoping to have her son baptized before the transfer to psychiatric care. The chaplain asked if she could sit, which was agreed to, and then the chaplain made a long speech to the effect that baptism is usually done in the context of a religious community except in a case of imminent death. The chaplain questioned the urgency of the request as well as the appropriateness of the setting. Blah blah blah.

Finally, the mother explained that they had been church shopping, attending both a nearby Catholic Church, and also a Methodist Church, and that her son did not like the Catholic priest, and made fun of his English language skills.

Then the grandmother appeared and after introductions told Paul to stop banging his head against the bed, as he had been doing throughout the visit, the chaplain seemingly oblivious. The chaplain then recommended they continue working with the Catholic Church and offered to help make arrangements. She then offered to make some prayers or blessings——or something to mark the transition. The mother replied, "Yes...anything." The chaplain added that she would pray for her as well.

Mother: "Right now, we just feel...I guess we feel like God is just too busy for us right now...and Paul said he feels like God does not like him right now because he's sick."

The chaplain explained that she would do some prayers, blessings, and rituals. "Whatever you want to do would be good," said the mother.

The chaplain then explained to Paul how this would be like going to church. Paul replied by mocking the priest, saying he could not understand him. "The peace of the Lord be 'whit chu,'" he mimicked the priest. Then Paul's sitter (a person assigned by the hospital to monitor the patient and prevent self-harm) piped up with an account of how her priest sounded like he was saying, "Piss the peace." Paul laughed.

After this bit of ribaldry, the chaplain went into her prayer ritual, under protest from Paul. But he settled down as the sitter held his feet still. He was informed that all he had to do was listen.

After some further pleasantries, the chaplain organized all present to lay hands on Paul and bless him while he giggled. All crossed themselves at the end of a long prayer of more than 200 words. The chaplain added that she would say a prayer for Paul every day of his hospitalization. (I doubt anyone could take that to the bank.)

Reflecting on her work here, which the chaplain describes as brief, she shows herself to be sophisticated enough to cite psychoanalytic concepts that might relate to this case theoretically. She quotes Winnicott and Rizzuto on matters of traditional objects and God-concepts, but how these psychoanalytic theories apply specifically to this case is left unstated. The chaplain says she was careful not to tie a masculine-parental image to God in her prayer. Finally, she encouraged the mother to pursue the baptism route to build collaboration with other religious leaders.

PUBLISHED CRITICAL RESPONSE OF HERBERT ANDERSON

Herbert Anderson is the first person assigned to provide a critical response to the use of rituals in work with patients. He notes that the ritual implemented by Chaplain Carole was perhaps "more than the mother had in mind." I quite agree. He further notes that there is a dearth of critical self-reflection on the part of this chaplain. He is eminently correct on both counts.

PUBLISHED CRITICAL RESPONSE OF MARK COBB

Mark Cobb questions the appropriateness of the extent to which the chaplain and staff touch this patient, seemingly against his wishes. He suggests, I think correctly, that physical touch might have been experienced as threatening to this troubled patient. On that point, I think he makes an important cautionary point. Cobb also asserts that the constraints of time prevented a more in-depth and more significant exploration of the problem in this family. But it was not the constraints of time that inhibited the chaplain. It was rather her woodenness in following literally the mother's request. The time was invested in attempting to satisfy the ritual request, rather than, say, a serious inquiry into the tragic history of this family. To be sure, time was said to be short, but that process might at least have been started, with possible good results.

MY CRITICAL RESPONSE

I first applaud the chaplain for her recognition of the potential value of reflecting on this case using psychoanalytic dynamics. But I do not think it suffices to cite a couple of psychoanalytic authorities in passing, filed by title, as she has done. I am not persuaded that Winnicott and Rizzuto are all that relevant at this preliminary stage of the relationship. But a more useful reference might have been an account of how the two cited theorists' ideas might relate to this particular family. That would take some thought, and the conclusion might be that there was no obvious connection. So is the chaplain simply name-dropping? We don't know.

Furthermore, the bedrock principle of psychoanalytic thought, to which we are all indebted, is the value of the patient doing the talking until the picture becomes more clear. But so far, in this case, the chaplain has done most of the talking, virtually all of it. The chaplain talks and prays, and designs ersatz rituals, effectively subverting her potential for playing a therapeutic role. Resorting to prayers and quasi-Catholic rituals is ill advised. There is no evidence that it might be therapeutic. In fact, it is rather silly. The chaplain is not even a Catholic herself, and thus looks out of place, incompetent, and illegitimate. She recommends a church with a priest whom the mother's troubled son is already mocking. And since the mother is church shopping, why, being a Protestant, would she hype Catholicism? More to the point, why does she hype any church when the only immediately available help for this troubled family is already in the room in the form of the chaplain?

The chaplain introduced herself using her first name, "Hi. I'm Jessica." This introduction puts her in a weak position from the start. The chaplain is not there to find a new friend. She has a problematic professional role to fulfill with a very troubled family. She has a very serious task and precious little time to accomplish anything. She needs to keep in full view her burden of sorting out how this family can be helped, if they can be helped at all. A first-name introduction relinquishes a considerable amount of her professional authority. No physician would enter a patient's room, "Hi. I'm Suzi Q." Nor should a clinical chaplain.

For all her bona fides, I do not think the chaplain served this family well. But let me first say that I am not sure that I or anyone else ultimately could have done much better. Here you have a mother and son, each with a psychiatric diagnosis, an abusive, absent father, and a disturbed son who is mocking religious authorities. Now enter the chaplain, another religious authority: a grim picture indeed. The prospects for serious help for this family in the course of an hour, are in my view extremely dim at best.

I think that a quiet chaplain, seated and listening for the entire hour, asking pertinent questions about the nature of this mother's painful journey, would be altogether quite enough, and potentially even therapeutic. This mother undoubtedly has a lot to tell. The chaplain could easily have opted out of any religious rite because this is a hospital, and there is little time, and she does not represent the Catholic religion that the mother might seem to prefer—not to mention the intrusive sitter present. As it turned out, the chaplain's choice of a mix of Catholic and Protestant religious practices seems to me to have been overdone to the point of being silly, and perhaps even quite confusing, to this troubled family. The ten-year-old patient's mockery of the priest's diction, seconded by the sitter, may have been the only voice of stark reality in this entire visit.

A significant, perhaps fatal, difficulty with employing sacred rituals in clinical pastoral work is that various religious rituals express many different and often conflicting values. Even two branches of Christianity, Protestant and Catholic, are adversaries in this particular matter. The chaplain's attempt at syncretism does not work.

How would this Protestant chaplain negotiate the other non-Christian religions? It gets very complicated. Is this chaplain also going to sprinkle holy water on the Shivalingam when she visits a Hindu patient, or chant "there is no God but Allah" when she visits a Muslim? Or attempt to blend them into a religious mélange?

A clinical chaplain should be as disengaged as possible from any of the symbols of any religion. An authentic pastoral clinician suspends his or her own beliefs, becoming a functional atheist, as no god is a part of the clinical world, and no god can be clinically assessed. However, human care is indeed part of the clinical world. The gift of listening belongs to the clinical world and is the possession of no particular religion. The chaplain in this case might have done well if she had known that and acted on it. Instead, she forgets that she is a clinician and poses instead as a religious functionary.

Rather than making the sign of the cross, tainting herself by acting like a Catholic, which she is not, and at the same time mouthing a long, ad-libbed Protestant prayer which likely edified no one, it would have been far better for her to sit and listen to the anguish of this desperate, on-edge mother. Surely the mother has much to say, if only someone would listen. She is not likely able to procure the services of a good psychiatrist unless she is well-fixed financially, or has good insurance. But a competent pastoral clinician might well have sat with her, asked her how these problems began, inquired about her broken marriage, other family stories, and whatever else might have come up. The result of that could have been, with a little luck, characterized as the talking cure. Everyone longs to talk, especially to a competent, intelligent listener. Chaplain Jessica Bratt Carle might have been that person, but instead, she drowned herself and the pastoral visit in waters of religious busywork. She failed the patient.

No, it isn't God who is too busy to help this broken family. It is the chaplain who is too busy—or perhaps merely insensitive, or worse, inept.

CASE 6
CONNECTING FAMILY MEMBERS
THROUGH RITUAL

Chaplain Gudlaug Helga Asgeirsdottir

Jacob, Hulda, and their family in palliative care

This case presents a sequence of religious rituals performed under the administration of Chaplain Asgeirsdottir in Iceland. The chaplain herself is well educated, with a doctoral degree in theology and training as a family therapist. She is a pastor ordained by the Evangelical Lutheran Church of Iceland, to which three-fourths of the population of Iceland belongs. She functions as a chaplain in the largest hospital in Iceland,

In this case, a dying patriarch named Jacob wanted to witness the baptism of his grandson before he died. There is no evidence that the family was active in the church or subscribed to the tenets of the church. That likely accounts for the fact that the hospital chaplain performed the baptism rather than a parish cleric. The liturgy of the baptism itself was temporarily halted at one point due to Jacob's respiratory difficulties, but continued subsequently without incident.

When Jacob died shortly after that, the chaplain was called by the hospital staff. She met the family gathered there, embraced them, and inquired about the process and how they had experienced Jacob's death. She then conducted a bedside service with Bible readings, prayers, and a blessing. It is not clear that the family wanted this. It seemed more like a hospital and cultural expectation. Incongruously, the chaplain thanked the family for the time she had with them and informed them that she planned to be with them at the burial of the ashes. Shouldn't they be thanking her? And shouldn't the family be asking her if she could be available for the burial?

At the service for the burial of ashes, there was a revolt. The family expressed its discontent with the burial site that was selected. The procedure was halted while the chaplain negotiated with the funeral-home worker. A new grave was chosen, and the family gave their consent. After the service, the chaplain was invited to the family home for refreshments, which she accepted.

Subsequently, the chaplain had several phone conversations and face-to-face meetings with the widow, who expressed in strong language her dissatisfaction with the healthcare professionals. She complained of not being listened to and that the patient had not been given adequate care. The widow felt that she had been denied the bereavement process. This seems likely to have been an oblique critique of the chaplain herself.

In her assessment of the case, Chaplain Asgeirsdottir judged that the rituals that she participated in with the family were "a powerful tool" that helped the family face this significant change in their lives. She concluded that the rituals were meaningful to them. She judged that the use of her Christian faith with the family provided them strength, comfort, and support. She concluded that the rituals helped to "soften the family members' anguish and despair by strengthening their inner resources and their network." The chaplain and the family appeared to be singing from different hymn books. Nevertheless, the chaplain concludes, as Pollyanna might, that "the family members' request for rituals could be interpreted as their inner need for something that could give them meaning and substance and be of value for them at this time in their lives."

PUBLISHED CRITICAL RESPONSE OF HERBERT ANDERSON

Anderson again assesses the chaplain as uncritical. She fulfilled without any questions the request for baptism. But in reality, as Anderson suggests, the appeal may have been rooted more in the connotation of what used to be labeled a "christening" or a "naming" ceremony. That would have been a more straightforward process, one that could have been done without much falderal, and without water, and may well have satisfied the dying patriarch. And the more complicated baptism, if the family were interested in such, could be left until later. Give Anderson an A.

PUBLISHED CRITICAL RESPONSE OF MARK COBB

Cobb takes a more optimistic view of the angry outburst in this family, seeing their willingness to give voice to anger as a sign of trust. Perhaps, but I am not persuaded, as the data does not suggest intimacy or significant trust between the chaplain and the family. To me it has the look of long-repressed anger, which may well still reside with the family.

MY CRITICAL RESPONSE

As a similarly distant reader of the documents and not as an observer of the process, I have the impression of a family wanting to honor their patriarch by staging a baptism of his new grandson at the bedside of said patriarch. Aside from that, I have an impression of a family system going along for the ride and perhaps thinking that this is just the way things are done around death and funerals. I saw no evidence in the reported material that the family in any way bought into anything. And finally, at the burial site, they revolted, making their voice heard to the effect that they were not, ultimately, going to buy into all this. At that point, the chaplain very appropriately took charge of a renegotiation, which seemed to satisfy them—temporarily. All that last-minute hoopla was, of course, the question of the location of the gravesite for the ashes. I suggest that the burial site ruckus was displaced discomfort, and subsequent events seem to support such a view, since later the family vigorously complained of their treatment overall. While the family did not directly implicate the chaplain, but rather the larger health system itself, it is not plausible that the family distinguished between the very established chaplain, the very established church, and the rest of the establishment. One gets the impression of an alienated family and perhaps an unresponsive church and/or medical establishment.

In some sense, this was not a clinical case at all, except at the end. By definition, a clinical case focuses attention on the body, as the derivation from the Greek *klinē* (bed) suggests—which is to say the body in bed, or the patient, or the client. Attending to the body requires listening and observing as opposed to talking, and as opposed to the introduction of unexplained theoretical programs or agendas. Throughout this case, the chaplain does not function as a clinician, but rather as a functionary of the hospital, the church, and the state. However, at the burial site, when she encountered anger from the family members, she did respond clinically.

The anger did seem overwrought; one might assume that it was the flowering of accumulated anger derived from something else. The something else may be related to their earlier passivity, matched with the chaplain's propensity to be directive.

To propose a reenactment of this case from a more clinical perspective, the chaplain might have met the family at the death scene in a taciturn manner, with relative silence, and inquired what, if anything, they might want from her in the way of assistance. We do not know, of course, what they might say, or whether they could speak with one voice. Working with groups is a particular hazard in and of itself. However, at the very least, the chaplain would then have put the family on notice that she elected to listen to them and to meet their expressed needs insofar as she was able. It appears from the write-up that the chaplain was hell-bent on doing her own thing, or rather the church and state thing, with the traditional prayers and blessings and all that. Thus she steam-rolled ahead.

In light of all this, one has to wonder what this chaplain would do with the death of a Jew, Muslim, Hindu, and so on. Perhaps she would be forced into the more productive role of inquiring what the family's wishes were and then listening like a pastoral psychotherapist.

In conclusion, Chaplain Agiersdottir writes, "the family members' request for rituals could be interpreted as their inner need for something that could give them meaning and substance and be of value for them at this time in their lives." Maybe, but the chaplain offers that claim without any supporting clinical data. I too cherish certain kinds of liturgies. They are a brand of art that sometimes inspires the heart. But I do not seek liturgies for every stressful situation. And one does not need clinical training to be a liturgist or to appreciate liturgy. It is a different kind of calling. Furthermore, there are an abundance of liturgists, but there is no abundance of competent pastoral clinicians or pastoral psychotherapists. They are very scarce.

A reading of this case suggests a family wishing to honor their dying patriarch, which they accomplished through the service of the chaplain. However, subsequently they appear to have been passive and generally unhappily participating in rituals that, for whatever reason, did not address their needs. I suggest that they would have welcomed a pastoral psychotherapeutic presence rather than the multiple liturgical exercises. In this case, we will never know. The chaplain's training as a family therapist is not demonstrated.

CASE 7
"I DO WANT TO GET
THIS FUNERAL PLANNED"

By Chaplain Patricia Roberts

Daisy, a former colleague in hospice care

The titular words here are from Daisy, a nurse in her mid-sixties working in the same hospital as Chaplain Roberts, who had been only recently employed there. Daisy was dying of an aggressive form of cancer. The chaplain reports that she sought to meet the needs presented her, rather than attempting to impose her own spiritual stance on her colleague. Daisy worked in the same hospital for thirty years and worked her way up to senior management. She was known for her optimism and generosity.

The chaplain describes herself as a mid-fifty-year-old Disciples of Christ minister with a Master of Divinity degree. Encountering Daisy at hospital meetings, she assumed that she might need some support. She appeared somewhat debilitated from the effects of the cancer, appearing aged. But she confessed to her dire condition with aplomb, unembarrassed.

In her account of the case, Chaplain Roberts interjects what she learned from reading pastoral clinician James E. Dittes: "The pastoral counselor witnesses—steadfastly, undistracted, relentlessly—the life experience of the counselee, the harried pilgrimage of a soul that has too often scurried in shadow. Lucid listener, the counselor beholds what has been averted, attests to what has been dismissed, hopes, and shames alike" (Dittes, 2005, p. 137; I suspect, however, that she is referring to *Pastoral Counseling: The Basics*, published in 1999). Dittes was one of the best. So Chaplain Roberts begins her work with excellent bona fides.

In hallway conversations, Daisy seemed to be telling the chaplain that she was not going to live too long. The two continued their relationship with such brief encounters. The chaplain then concluded that she needed to carve out space for Daisy to share more seriously her downward journey. Daisy seemed not to take the bait.

Some of the staff brought religious tracts to Daisy, explaining how she might "get right with the Lord." Daisy herself had blessedly little patience with Evangelicals, who were concerned about her soul. Some of the staff expressed concern as well about Daisy's long-term relationship with a particular physician, an Indian national of Sikh background who professed atheism. In this context, the chaplain felt it her mission to give support to Daisy as a counter to the ambient religious and moral pressures abounding in their institution—all the marks of American small-town narrow-minded morality and religiosity.

Daisy remained somewhat distant. After all, an institutional chaplain does not normally step into the pastoral therapeutic role in relation to colleagues, particularly those above her in the chain of command. That is dangerous territory, changing the terms of the implied chaplaincy contract. Chaplain Roberts was thus on soft ground. The chaplain took two weeks leave from her job for surgery of her own at the end of the year, and when she returned, Daisy had retired and disappeared. Neither woman reached out to the other. Three months later, they saw each other briefly at a wedding. They had eye contact, but Daisy slipped away before Chaplain Roberts could connect with her. Three weeks later, word came to the chaplain that Daisy had entered hospice and wanted a visit from Chaplain Roberts. Connecting with Daisy and getting directions to her home was difficult, but she finally reached a daughter who informed the chaplain that Daisy wanted her to do the funeral.

When she finally met with Daisy at her home, Daisy declared some broad ideas of what she wanted at her funeral. "I'm dying," she confessed. She was agitated. She also revealed to the chaplain that her husband of seven years was in denial, and they had been fighting. Daisy seemed to want to discuss the problem with her husband more than she wanted to discuss the projected funeral. Unaccountably, and perhaps inappropriately, the chaplain was frustrated by this, feeling she needed more direction about Daisy's wishes regarding the funeral. The chaplain errs here, showing more interest in getting the funeral correct than in attending to the patient's concerns. The patient was focused on the "living" process of dying. The chaplain was concerned about the funeral.

Visiting a week later, Chaplain Roberts found Daisy in further decline, and what was new was her request for prayer. She shared more ideas of her wishes for the funeral, which to the chaplain sounded more like a wedding than a funeral. Her bed had been moved to the sunroom so that Daisy could view the flowers outside. Daisy and her daughter were now requesting no visitors. Cards would suffice.

In the third visit, a week later, Daisy related how her special friend, Dr. Singh, had come for dinner the night before and had brought a splendid array of flowers with a red rose in the middle to signify Daisy. They had discussed reincarnation, which Daisy found comforting. Singh had talked to her about reincarnation. They reminisced, with Daisy doing most of the talking. Daisy requested no memorial service at the hospital but insisted that everyone should be invited to the funeral at her beach house, which would be catered so that all her friends could eat without having to work. She was intent on getting the funeral planned. At the close of this third visit, Daisy asked for prayer for only the second time in their relationship.

The fourth visit was a few days later, as Daisy was in further decline. She chose two popular songs for the funeral that her special grandson Joshua favored. The chaplain had heard of neither and was a little troubled about the sexually explicit language in them, but she decided not to comment. Daisy had had a special relationship with that particular grandson, who himself had some kind of handicap and a father who had been an addict. Daisy also agreed to a couple of traditional hymns, and it was clear to the chaplain that Daisy knew her church's hymnbook, citing the page number of hymns she did *not* want to be sung.

A few days later, the chaplain made her fifth visit. Daisy had picked out three songs for the funeral, two for the special grandson, the ones with sexually explicit language, and one for her husband. Daisy also had two hymns she wanted but indicated again that there were others commonly used that she did not want.

Four days later, the chaplain made her sixth home visit. Daisy was weaker. She talked and nodded. In response to Daisy's question "Why is this happening to me?" the chaplain slipped into a mini-sermon about the character of God that was of questionable appropriateness or value. But Daisy thanked her, adding, "Do you think that it is time that I allow them to give me morphine so I can rest?" The implied answer that she sought was "yes." A week later, Daisy's husband called to say she was dying and asked if the chaplain could come and pray. She went, and shortly after she left Daisy on this visit, Daisy died. Chaplain Roberts presided at the funeral.

Except for some banal quote to the effect that the living are defined by whom they have lost, a transcript of the funeral sermon is not provided. Nor is there any verbatim text of the Chaplain's prayers. They might have been helpful in assessing the quality of the chaplain's work. What a chaplain says in prayers can be revelatory.

The chaplain summarized her work with Daisy, declaring it to have been "an aesthetic witness, as someone bearing witness to the story of the deceased," and Daisy herself had done the work. I should think that "pastoral therapeutic presence" would have been a more appropriate moniker for the chaplain's contribution, especially if one has delved into James Dittes and his ilk. Chaplain Roberts assessed her work as having provided support, without pressure to conform to any particular religious expression. The summary seems accurate. The chaplain expressed concern, to herself, about the songs with sexually explicit language dedicated to the grandson, but she complied with Daisy's wishes, blessedly. Daisy wanted her funeral to be a celebratory event, and apparently it was that. The chaplain declared that the final celebration was not a religious ceremony, but that depends on how one defines religion. I would say that it was as religious as anything is religious. Finally, she concluded that the relationship with Daisy strengthened her role in the hospital community and earned her newfound trust in that community, a quite credible claim.

An issue never touched upon was the problem for institutional chaplains attempting to minister to people in administration or ranked above them. Daisy had not been the chaplain's direct administrator, but she was in administration. It is dangerous and risky territory. However, all's well that ends well.

PUBLISHED RESPONSE OF HERBERT ANDERSON

Anderson rightly questions the appropriateness of Chaplain Robert's extensive therapeutic involvement with this hospital staff person, suggesting that the task of working with Daisy's dying and death belongs elsewhere, presumably to a parish cleric. Anderson is surely correct in principle. In the world, as we once knew it in our youth, no hospital chaplain would assume the intensive role that Chaplain Roberts assumed with a dying staff person, particularly one in administration, to whom the chaplain was implicitly and to some extent accountable. But the world has changed. Chaplaincy has changed. The boundary markers have been moved, and no one is quite sure exactly where they are now.

Anderson also questions who is paying the bill here. Is Chaplain Roberts "on the clock," as we say, in her work with Daisy, or is she volunteering her time? My rejoinder to Anderson's very appropriate question, again, is that our world has changed. Boundaries are fuzzier, and it is only going to get worse. Fewer people have membership in religious communities in which religious leaders filled this role in the past. But for Roberts to decide that Daisy's death was not her business, I think, would have been callous. Anderson is not exactly wrong. He provides a cautionary note. It may be a matter of asking the hospital to revise Chaplain Roberts' job description.

PUBLISHED CRITICAL RESPONSE OF MARK COBB

Cobb makes a positive comment on Chaplain Roberts' work with Daisy and does not register any critical questions.

MY CRITICAL RESPONSE

I prefer strong critiques. One strong critique is typically all one ever gets to make on a clinical case, like do or die. For this clinical case, I give a firm and definite "job well done." The chaplain seemed to learn well from James Dittes, a significant authority in clinical pastoral care and counseling, or pastoral psychotherapy. Dittes, alas, died in 2009.

If I am required to point to minor weaknesses or failures in this case, I will say that the funeral sermon, or what little of it is shared in the write-up, was a tad insipid. I also thought the chaplain was a bit too nervous about the sexual lyrics in the songs requested by Daisy to honor her grandson. After all, love, as they say, is the only argument against death. I believe it was Tillich who gave us that. And the biblical Song of Songs, in ancient times an orgiastic funeral ritual, is astonishingly erotic, and of course, seldom heard in church, undoubtedly for that very reason. Come to think of it, Daisy, if I know her from Chaplain Robert's account, would likely have rejoiced to have had the Song of Songs read in full at her funeral, or sung, and perhaps even preached upon. The sermon might have been much better than whatever the chaplain preached. And it would have gone nicely with her grandson's sexually explicit music. But the chaplain missed that one.

As for Chaplain Roberts' two prayers at the bedside of the dying Daisy, said at Daisy's request, I regret that the chaplain does not provide us a verbatim account. It would be interesting to note whether the prayers were in the voice of Daisy or the voice of the chaplain. Hopefully, they were in the voice of the former. If the latter, I would be sorry. A consistent clinician, in my view, does not merely offer a prayer. The clinician asks what kind of prayer the supplicant wants to make. As such, the prayers are the patient's prayers. Then the clinician may assent or not, of course.

In any case, Chaplain Roberts acquitted herself quite well overall, especially in her several one-to-one visits with Daisy. She presented herself mostly as a listener. Blessedly, there was no "come to Jesus" injunction. She made some connections. She did not talk too much overall, a common flaw in virtually all clergy. And she demonstrated heart. Unfortunately, we are not provided the verbal content of the bedside prayers and the sermon, which may well have undermined the entire pastoral project. That aside, you don't see much better pastoral psychotherapeutic presence than in this case of Chaplain Roberts.

CASE 8
"FOR MYSELF AND FOR YOUR PEOPLE WHOM I PRAY"

By Rabbi Amy E. Goodman and Chaplain Joel Baron

Mrs. Pearlman, an eighty-two-year-old woman with a terminal diagnosis of advanced Alzheimer's disease

The patient, Mrs. Pearlman, also had co-morbid conditions of coronary artery disease and diabetes mellitus. Her decline was marked by anorexia, weight loss, decreased ability to engage, increased daytime sleepiness, and increased pain. She was entirely dependent on others for ambulation, transfer, dressing, bathing, toileting, and feeding. She had behavioral disturbances and hallucinations.

Mrs. Pearlman rarely declined an offer of a blessing from people of any religion. The case study here presented involves her relationship with the primary hospice chaplain, Rabbi Jacobs. Early in the relationship, Mrs. Pearlman tearfully expressed her view that she was being "called home." But it was a beautiful place where "God saw all people as beautiful inside and out." In response, the rabbi offered various Hebrew prayers, lit Shabbat candles for her, blessed her with the Birka Kohanim, and kissed her on the forehead. Then they had a brief conversation about the food of High Holy Days. Then she got tired. But even so, the rabbi offered a brief High Holy Day ritual of about twenty minutes, followed by other Jewish liturgical songs and prayers. In conclusion, the rabbi placed his hands on Mrs. Pearlman's head for yet another blessing in both Hebrew and English. Then he departed with another blessing.

I presume that Mrs. Pearlman appreciated the attention and the religious rites. Still, it seems to me to have been quite extended, particularly for a person with advanced Alzheimer's disease who has a limited attention span. The rabbi concluded that Mrs. Pearlman was profoundly engaged and extremely expressive emotionally, though non-verbally, throughout his extended visit. She frequently smiled and hummed the parts of familiar refrains of the prayers. And she was frequently tearful.

The pastoral care professional in this case is a fictional Rabbi Jacobs, who seems to be a fabricated composite of two religious authorities, rabbis I believe, who invested the most time with Mrs. Pearlman.. The roles of Goodman and Baron are not anywhere described. The ministering rabbis are said to be anonymized in order to protect Mrs. Pearlman. Why she would need to be protected is a mystery not explained.

This is therefore a most peculiar clinical presentation. The patient seems to have been humored in the extreme and likely not very aware of what was taking place, except for the fact that she appreciated all the attention, and she seems to have received an inordinate amount of it.

In terms of gaining insight into clinical skills in delivering pastoral care and pastoral psychotherapy, I cannot see how this case contributes much of anything, except perhaps to laud the virtue of being kindly to the old and senile.

NEITHER HERBERT ANDERSON NOR MARK COBB MAKES CRITICAL COMMENTS ON THE PEARLMAN CASE

MY CRITICAL RESPONSE

I do not doubt that the rabbis' visits were comforting to this patient, who was in the late stages of Alzheimer's disease. Still, an aspect of this pastoral relationship is that it seems impossible to procure reliable feedback from the patient or to assess in any way what she was experiencing. From a clinical perspective, we simply would have to say that it cannot be known what Mrs. Pearlman took in or what her thoughts may have been. Thus critical commentary is difficult to make.

I do applaud the rabbis for their dedication to such afflicted people, but I believe it will be impossible to assess the value or appropriateness of their work. However, given the inordinate amount of time allocated to Mrs. Pearlman, and the current scarcity of resources in the wider community, the question of appropriate and wise distribution of resources must be examined. With all the neediness in the world, why is the choice made to concentrate so much time and attention on Mrs. Pearlman? She may well have been content with an occasional visit of only a few minutes. My conclusion is that the rabbis' excessive time and energy, or at least the bulk of it, could be more creatively used with troubled people who are alert, rational, and have both critical needs and something of a future. Mrs. Pearlman's life was virtually over. She likely understood little of what was said to her. The rabbis were kindly and generous, but human need abounds. One might conclude that they are investing their time and energy in a profligate manner. I surmise that a three-minute visit would have been just as useful to Mrs. Pearlman as the significantly extended time that the rabbis gave to her. If that surmise can be shown to be accurate, the chaplain-rabbis are misallocating resources.

I also find the reference to "your people" a bit jarring. Is this an allusion to Jewish and Christian exclusivism? If so, it should be reconsidered. On the other hand, I suppose it could be exegeted to be a reference to all obedient people, which I would take to be appropriate. And we all know that Judaism is consistently universalistic, even if such universalism is often betrayed in practice.

Once again, however, any search in this case for the much-touted measurable and evidence-based outcomes will inevitably come up empty-handed.

CASE 9
"I'D LIKE YOU TO GET TO KNOW ABOUT ME."

Chaplain Steve Nolan, Co-Editor

*Kristof, a fifty-year-old atheist academic admitted to a hospice
for palliative symptom control*

In the monograph under review, of which he is co-editor, Steve Nolan himself presents a case in which he himself functions as a chaplain in the hospice where he is employed. Nolan's partnering editor, George Fitchett, did not present a case of his own. In their previous joint effort, also reviewed by me, neither man presented any of his own work. Thus Nolan is clearing new ground, and deserves applause.

This case describes Nolan's work with a dying man who is assigned a pseudonym, as is the practice in each of the published clinical cases. This man is given the pseudonym "Kristof."

In the introduction to the monograph, Nolan set the context by confessing in the first paragraph quite candidly that "spiritual" care was impervious to definition: "The lack of an agreed-upon and plainly articulated definition for spiritual care means that, as a profession, chaplains struggle to explain clearly the nature of the work." I found this admission refreshing and honest, and I welcome Nolan to the world of candor and honesty. It is a very small world. Obviously Nolan's assertion conforms to my personal experience as well, that spiritual and spirituality are categories of uncertain boundaries, amorphous and without definition. However, we can indeed assess the pastoral rather than the spiritual quality of a case, and we can also evaluate a case from a psychoanalytic perspective, as well we should.

Kristof was admitted to a hospice for palliative symptom control. His projected life span was a matter of several weeks. His medical notes recorded "No religious faith but would welcome chaplaincy support." Thus Nolan visited him. When he knocked and announced himself as a chaplain, Kristof immediately stood, offered a handshake, and then sat on the bed with his shoes on and back against the wall, leaving the single chair for Nolan. Kristof first explained that he was never free of pain. Nolan asked if he was all right with a visit, a seemingly unnecessary question at this point, and the reply was affirmative. Kristof added that he was not religious, but believed in a higher power, and respected other people's religion. "I'm not going to turn down any offer of help," he confessed. "I'm dying. I've had this thing for about a year. I've had chemo and radiotherapy, and I've probably got a few months left to live."

Nolan was rightly concerned that the opening moments of a relationship would likely be determinative, and also that he might be wrongly perceived as bearing a religious agenda. He was anxious that he might be rejected out of hand.

Thus Nolan said, "My role is to support people in their religious needs, if they have any, either directly or by liaising with others; but if a person isn't religious, my role is to support them in whatever way I can." So Nolan presented a very sensible outline of his philosophy of pastoral care. However, I had the sense from reading the case that he was guilding the lily, because his rationale about visiting had already been communicated non-verbally. But of course I was not there, and Nolan was.

Kristof then revealed that he is in the hospital because he took an overdose in a failed suicide attempt. He said he was in unmanageable pain. Nolan attempted to make it clear that he made no judgments about the morality of suicide.

Kristof then disclosed that he would like help in understanding who he had been and what his life had meant. He wanted to understand that with respect to Christianity. "I'd like you to get to know me," he said.

So the pastoral relationship was established quite quickly, and with potential for profundity and intimacy.

Nolan then notes that he was struck by how Kristof seemed to be looking directly at dying without flinching. Kristof replied that he did not want to do this all the time, and then he disclosed how he had prepared for his demise. He had already allocated his estate to his wife, from whom he was separated, and their children.

In closing the first visit, Nolan again offered to assist him. It seems that Nolan is a bit self-effacing and unnecessarily humble here. The record strongly suggests that Kristof had already appointed Nolan as his pastoral consultant. So again, Kristof affirmed that he would like to work with Nolan, that he would look forward to it. "I think we'll get along well," he concluded. A quite blessed beginning.

The second session was almost a week later. Kristof's medical regimen made it challenging to meet at times convenient to both Nolan and Kristof. When they finally met, Kristof was relaxed, welcoming, and ready to talk. Kristof told of his deciding against surgery because of its very poor prognosis and the likelihood of its causing additional pain.

The subject of suicide came up again, and Nolan made clear again his non-judgmental approach. Kristof then offered a short discourse on the Church and its fire and brimstone attack on suicide. Then Kristof confessed that he was tired, but that he wanted eventually to talk about more personal matters, like how he could face his death. But he added, "I think we've hit it off...we seem to see things the same way."

The third visit, four days later, was brief. Kristof's speech was unclear at times. But he spoke again of wanting to understand himself better before he died.

The fourth visit, three days later, was challenging to process. Kristof's speech was even less decipherable. He struggled to articulate the word "cynical" but finally wrote it in his notebook for Nolan to read. Then he smiled and said, "I feel like I'm on holiday in Albania." Nolan was not able to follow him. Nolan spoke about how we can think about God and whether God exists, but that went nowhere. Kristof elaborated about how he spent time making an inventory of his life——like counting cups and saucers. Finally, Kristof concluded that he achieved some things in life. Nolan then shared some of his struggles to achieve, coming as he does from a working-class family. Kristof paid little attention. The two seemed to talk past each other for a bit. The content of the conversation seemed disjointed. It appears that Nolan's decision to self-disclose was distracting and was not of interest to Kristof. I had the impulse to ride a fairy to Nolan and whisper in his ear, "Shut up." But the simple fact that the two were in the same room conversing——and apparently relating—was probably a blessing to Kristof in spite of Nolan's somewhat ill-timed verbosity. The significant takeaway here is that Kristof wanted Nolan to listen, and was not much interested in Nolan's own story. This is an example of the most common error of chaplains and pastors everywhere. They want to talk about or promote their own religions or themselves personally. The therapeutic work of listening to the patient and making connections is abandoned.

The fifth meeting occurred a week later. Though Nolan had encountered Kristof occasionally around the halls of the hospital, catching him alone in his room was difficult. His estimated life expectancy was now "up to eight weeks." In this meeting, Kristof left the television war movie on, with the sound off, while he talked to Nolan. Nolan was struck by the fact that in this visit, Kristof never looked him in the face as he talked about suicide; he would use morphine. The hospital staff was tolerant, Kristof said, and he was at peace. Kristof talked about preferring an analytic kind of Christian, one who could discuss and decide for himself what he believes. Then, to Nolan's amazement, Kristof added that for him, there was one non-negotiable belief: in the resurrection and in Jesus as the son of God. "I'll find out in eight weeks," said Kristof. The conversation lasted over an hour. (Wait a minute. This guy was saying he's an atheist and now this?) Kristof perhaps had not distinguished between agnosticism and atheism. But at that stage of his life, did it matter?

After the hour, Kristof commented, "That was an interesting discussion. You picked a good moment today." It is noteworthy that the conversation consisted of Kristof talking and Nolan listening, without eye contact, and with the TV running silently. It was almost as if Kristof organized willy-nilly a replica of Freud's consultation room, where the patient talks and the therapist remains mostly silent and out of sight. The silent TV seems to have created the atmosphere that enabled the patient to avoid eye contact with Nolan by providing an alternate focal point. And the record shows that Kristof did most of the talking, and that he himself directed the course of the conversation, as should be the case in such attempts at pastoral psychotherapy. This visit seems to have been the high point of the pastoral relationship. It seems almost that Kristof forced Nolan to be a competent psychotherapist. Kudos to Nolan for allowing himself to act with competence.

The sixth visit was five days later. Since the previous visit, plans had been made for Kristof's discharge. He was packed and ready. Nolan came to say goodbye. Kristof confessed that he was edgy about moving on, although he might have been tense about the possibility of losing contact with Nolan. Kristof brought up resurrection again, saying it was something he had never understood. Nolan mentioned Archbishop Romero, who was assassinated by government operatives in San Salvador, and what an inspiration he was to the poor. Nolan commented in his notes that he brought up the archbishop's fate as a way to suggest that the archbishop's life had been an inspiration to others. Kristof countered, saying that there had been nothing inspirational in his own life, seeming to reject the analogy. Nolan recognized that he was making an ill-conceived attempt at rescuing Kristof. After some banter, Nolan added that he thought it a matter of perspective. "Mmm, I don't have any perspective," said Kristof. Chaplain and patient ended this visit in a kind of cordial opposition. Nolan had slipped somewhat out of his therapeutic role and into a brief bit of sermonizing. But his slip did not seem to have breached the relationship. Kristof seemed to reject every Pollyanna offering that Nolan put forward, which says a lot about both Kristof and Nolan and their ability to communicate.

As they parted, Kristof said, "When I've settled in, perhaps you'll come and see me; in fact, I'd actively welcome you to come and see me. I'll be more focused. I'm a bit distracted today. I'd like to talk more about Christianity. I don't know much about it."

Nolan saw Kristof four more times over the next three weeks. Those visits seemed to be in an adjunct facility. Alas, he does not provide detailed data on those visits. I wish he had. Nolan reports that he wanted to offer him time and space to work on himself, but it seems that that did not happen because Kristof was too distracted. Kristof was then readmitted to the hospital. When Nolan telephoned to arrange a visit, he was informed that Kristof had just died of a sudden bleed.

PUBLISHED CRITICAL RESPONSE OF CHERYL HOLMES

The psychiatric commentator Cheryl Holmes who follows up Nolan's write-up, nicely reinforces Nolan's assessment of his countertransference and the possibility that it led him to be less effective than he might have been. However, she owns that "might" is the determinative here. It is by no means clear that Nolan's countertransference was all that distracting to Kristof. There probably does not exist anywhere the perfectly modulated therapeutic relationship in which transference and countertransference together bring perfect understanding and healing. All human relationships are messy; no person, whether a therapist or not, can expect to relate to another with perfect awareness of the unconscious of both parties and to accomplish perfect modulation, to the end that distortion is eliminated. The blessed fact here, however, is that Nolan attends to this issue. Attending to issues is most of the battle. And no one can expect to come out unscathed.

PUBLISHED CRITICAL RESPONSE OF LINDA EMANUEL

The second psychiatric commentator, Linda Emanuel, in what may be the most brilliant essay in the monograph, commends Nolan as one psychiatrist willing to expose his work among the many preferring only to look good. Emanuel offers a quite informative description of countertransference. She closes her remarks by wondering if Nolan allowed his countertransference to color too much his care of Kristof. She is not sure. But Emanuel wonders if perhaps he offered too much advice that was informed by his own journey, and thereby missed some things important to Kristof. She also adds that it is quite generous to admit one's therapeutic errors, even to the patient, a refreshing injunction. This essay, and the one above, are worth the price of the book.

MY CRITICAL RESPONSE

It must be said, unequivocally, that Nolan's care for Kristof was of unusually high quality. And in comparison with most of the other published clinical cases in this collection, as well as in the previous collection, this work was exemplary, especially in the fifth pastoral visit. Nolan was caring and self-reflective. He occasionally went off on his rants, talking instead of listening, too eager to share rather than listening to the patient. Still, in large part, he generously made himself available to Kristof with understanding and compassion. And he blessedly made no move to impose prayer or other religious rituals on Kristof.

As reported by Nolan, there were aspects of Kristof's presentation of himself that were impenetrable. For one, the seemingly agnostic Kristof flip-flopped on the matter of what he believed religiously. This agnostic academic at points began to present himself as something close to a Christian fundamentalist. This unexpected turn to conventional Christian belief caught the chaplain off balance, as it likely would have anyone. That was quite understandable. An agnostic, scientifically-oriented man, subscribing at the last hour to conventional Christian belief, has the look of someone hedging his bets. At the same time, I thought Nolan put too much weight on the matter, which is part of the countertransference. It could have been that Kristof was attempting to ingratiate himself with Nolan, the cleric. Besides that, what does it matter in one's last days what one believes about this or that doctrine, given that it is about to come out in the wash.

Nolan assessed his interventions with Kristof as a combination of reassurance and life review. I would not say that was inaccurate. However, I thought the salient aspect of Nolan's offering to Kristof was simply the presence of an intelligent, caring, and therapeutically oriented listener to Kristof at his point of dying. In that respect, I thought Nolan both wise and effective overall. However, at points Nolan was a bit too eager to offer reassurance, and in this case, reassurance rather external to Kristof, all of which Kristof seemed to reject. I also thought that Nolan was at times too quick to speak and too fast to bring up theological issues. Nobody's perfect.

Nolan is self-critical regarding his occasional efforts to reassure Kristof. I think he was correct in this bit of self-analysis. But Nolan also felt that he failed to assess and respond adequately to Kristof's spiritual needs, specifically in failing to explore what Kristof's life had meant concerning Christianity. I suggest that is a bridge too far. I see no value in trying to shoe-horn Kristof into the state religion, or into anything else at this point in his life. Isn't it enough that Kristof finds in Nolan a comrade who cares about him enough to listen to him and holds no brief against his self-described apostasy? To the extent Nolan accomplished that, I believe he incarnated the best of religion. Blessedly he did not press this matter of religious belief, even if at certain moments he sounded like a catechist, and even if Kristof himself sounded at times like an eager postulant. Or, put another way, Kristof's affective and analytical bond with Nolan was, in my view, all the Christianity Kristof needed at that extreme point at the end of his life. Doesn't love remain still the only argument against death?

On the question that Kristof openly raised for himself, whether his life had had any significance, he seemed to suggest a negative answer. But how can anyone authentically answer such a question? No one is that omniscient; furthermore, it certainly must be any thinking person's question at the end. But how could anyone know? Even Jesus himself could not know the answer to that question.

Finally, Nolan reflects on his countertransference and attempts to explore how his being with Kristof had affected him personally. Notably, Nolan asserts that this aspect of clinical training in Britain is typically neglected. Nolan states that the absence of a psychoanalytic perspective is a lacuna in what passes in Britain for clinical pastoral training. Finally, Nolan argues that this need for pastoral clinicians to reflect on their transferential issues is an urgent one in Britain. Nolan likely does not know the American scene well, but the issue is an urgent one here, too.

In a final and potent shot, Nolan challenges any turn to "outcomes" research among pastoral clinicians that bypasses the psychoanalytic perspective. We fully agree. And we encourage Nolan to have a come-to-Jesus meeting with his co-editor, George Fitchett, on this matter.

In a curious coda, Nolan suggests that his over-identification with Kristof resulted in his failure to help Kristof make sense of his life concerning Christianity. I think we should all thank God that Nolan failed to make Kristof a Christian. I do not see any fault there. Kristof found a fellow human being who invested time with him, listened, imposed no judgment on him, and seems to have affirmed—powerfully—Kristof's humanity. How could he have found anyone better?

So three cheers for Nolan. In his British culture, where Anton Boisen is unread and unknown, there does not seem to exist much awareness of the new thing that Boisen injected into American culture, namely that the competent pastor does mostly the same work that Sigmund Freud did, only from a somewhat different platform, and furthermore that competent pastors cannot afford to be unaware of their own psychological proclivities and their transferential issues. Nolan understands all that. Now we can hope that Nolan will be the one to start a Boisenite revolution in the United Kingdom. It's not too early!

AFTERWORD

George Fitchett and Steve Nolan have begun a new thing, the publication of clinical pastoral cases with attached critiques. Why that approach has not been previously attempted and embraced in the clinical pastoral field in this generation is a mystery. It is simple, and it is a process embedded in a century of clinical pastoral tradition at the local level. It is exactly the process that has taken place in clinical pastoral training programs locally for generations. For some mysterious reason, no one seems to have thought hitherto of publishing and distributing such cases publicly, at least not to my knowledge. Thus I hope this design is a signal of more to come.

While Fitchett and Nolan have created a promising new approach to understanding pastoral care, counseling, and psychotherapy, I fault them for lack of rigor. With a few exceptions, the published critiques have been quite thin. The purpose of this critical volume (and my previous one, *Nine Clinical Cases*) is to add a degree of seriousness, and undoubtedly at times malaise, to the conversation. The clinical pastoral profession as a whole cannot afford any longer to pull its punches as it evaluates its work. It cannot afford to let sloppy pastoral work escape severe criticism. The risk of doing so is that the entire field will degenerate further. Thus with these published critiques, I hope others will also be inspired to publish cases so that we may see more rigorous examinations of clinical pastoral work. The field of pastoral care, counseling, and psychotherapy will be thereby enriched.

Of the nine cases reviewed above, only two stand out to me as acceptably self-critical: those presented by Patricia Roberts and Steve Nolan. Since Nolan is one of the two editors, it is strange that he did not require the other cases to be subjected to the same rigorous critique he gave his own work. In my conversations with him, he did not have an answer for that. At least a part of the solution, I surmise, is that the clinical pastoral movement, originating in the U.S., has never yet established roots in Great Britain.

But in fact it does not matter much in the long run that a serious critical dimension is absent from most of the cases. All nine cases stand on their own, are interesting enough to attract readers, and are available for critique from any quarter. Criticism does not need to stop with this monograph. Of course I have taken advantage of the availability of the cases to make my criticisms. I hope that my observations will be learning experiences for all readers and that further conversation will be stimulated.

Case criticism can be made by the actors themselves, as Nolan has personally demonstrated. But in real life, astute criticism is more likely to come from the outside. Few people can see their errors and oversights as well as another can. Self-protection and self-delusion are common to us all.

APPENDIX I

CONTRA FITCHETT
THE TANGENTIAL MATTER OF
EVIDENCE-BASED OUTCOMES
or
GEORGE FITCHETT'S HOBBY HORSE

A Review of the Afterword
of
Case Studies in Spiritual Care

Entitled "Case Studies and Chaplaincy Research"

Co-editor George Fitchett makes a call in this book's afterword (and elsewhere) for more chaplaincy research focused primarily on chaplaincy outcomes and, as he puts it, evidence-based outcomes. He seems to be wanting to put pastoral care (or spiritual care, as he likes to call it) on the same playing field as scientific medicine. This thesis is is wrong-headed and is destined for the junk heap.

Research on clinical pastoral work exists for the most part in an entirely different arena from scientific medicine. In scientific medicine, one can propose treatment regimens, select patients, and test for effectiveness through double-blind studies, and in that way discover what works and what does not work. The process is very effective for evaluating drugs, types of surgery, and other methods of medical intervention. However, such a scientific approach does not work with pastoral care, counseling, psychotherapy, psychoanalysis, and even much of social work. It is wrong-headed to think so.

We indeed seek outcomes, and often see them, but the evidence supporting the alleged outcomes is often quite ephemeral, difficult to produce, and often impossible to cull. Sigmund Freud himself knew this and confessed that he never thought of himself as a real doctor. He viewed himself as "a secular pastoral worker."

The reason scientific protocols do not work in pastoral work (or in spiritual work either, whatever that is) is that credible testing of hypotheses is impossible and collecting the ephemeral supporting data equally problematic. Pastoral work is such an intangible undertaking that it does not submit to strict scientific scrutiny. Of course, there are methods of assessing competency, but they depend upon a certain amount of guessing and subjectivity.

How does one measure the value of a pastor sitting with a grieving widow for an hour or more, saying little or nothing? How does one rule out the possibility that the widow is simply humoring the pastor and waiting for him or her to leave?

If you have a dead body, with a bullet in the brain and a gun from which the bullet emerged, and fingerprints on the gun, you can argue with some degree of scientific credibility that you know what the victim died of and who killed him (if the owner of the fingerprints can be found). But in clinical pastoral work, there are no fingerprints to lift, no reliable witnesses to confirm this or that, no scientifically reliable tests that can be employed to authenticate assumptions——and usually no guns.

Clinical pastoral work, whether it is referred to as care, counseling, psychotherapy, or psychoanalysis, does not subject itself to typical, scientific research protocols. Its outcomes are elusive and difficult to test for. If such a process were workable, Freud and psychoanalysis would have long ago been scientifically judged to be either a fraudulent enterprise or a scientifically demonstrable method of medical treatment. But we know it is neither. Psychiatric treatment (except for its drug treatment division) and psychoanalysis, like pastoral work, are at best very soft sciences. Even the label "science" is arguably inappropriate.

Examining the nine cases of pastoral work in this Fitchett-Nolan book will not reveal one that could be appropriately subjected to scientifically-oriented research on the value of its outcomes. For that matter, you could probably not find one that could be subjected to concrete analysis of any sort. The outcomes in every case are, from a scientific perspective, fluid and uncertain. All that can be said is that a guess could be made that the pastoral work seemed to be effective or not effective. That does not make good science. An evidence-based outcome in the work of curing souls is an illusion.

APPENDIX II
AN EXAMINATION OF
THE NINE CASES INDIVIDUALLY,
IN SEARCH OF EVIDENCE-BASED
OUTCOMES

CASE 1

In the case of Mark, the eleven-year-old with brain cancer who was attended to by a caring female chaplain, he may or may not have benefited from the pastoral work. Since he was unable to speak, we would have to guess. The guess would be that since he liked the chaplain and seemed to look forward to her visits, he benefited in some way. Beyond that, we are left pretty much in the dark. But there is no evidence that the chaplain's visits were any more therapeutic than that of, say, the cleaning staff, if he had that.

The outcomes of the attention Mark received were likely to have been positive for him but "likely" is the governing word here. Mark's chaplains make the astonishing claim that with the chaplain, Mark connected and found "the presence of the transcendent—the wounded healer himself."

At best that is fanciful thinking, unsupported by any data. At worst it is psychotic thinking. To presume that Mark has found God is a trip much too far, to put it very gently. It is undoubtedly a claim over the top. Now, of course, we know that people sometimes mouth such pieties when their lives are turned upside down, or when they change their ways of living for the better. They may say things like "having found God," but they don't mean that literally. God, by definition, has never been lost—or found. What they mean is that they feel that God has called them to a different way of living, and that might be very good. But feelings cannot be measured or tested in a lab. They do not qualify as evidence-based outcomes.

Thus chaplains purporting to be clinicians working in a clinical environment like a hospital should never use such phrases as "finding God." If they do, they will be written off as psychotic and delusional—or perhaps merely religious fools. We cannot speak in such a manner in a clinical setting and expect to be taken seriously, even if some medical professionals do.

So what are the outcomes in this case? They are marginal and illusive. The patient seemed to like the chaplain, and the patient in his isolated world certainly needed someone to like, which for Mark could have been a happy outcome. To characterize Mark's seeming responsiveness to the chaplain as an evidence-based outcome is untenable.

CASE 2

In the case of the infant Sarah, diagnosed *in utero* with Trisomy 18 syndrome (meaning that her prognosis was so grim that some physicians recommended abortion), the outcomes are equally tenuous.

The family declined to opt for abortion. So the chaplain became involved, visited the family and patient during the half year of the infant's life, and was seemingly a significant comfort to them. It is not specified how much time the chaplain spent with the family. He describes only five encounters with the patient and/or parents over the six months of Sarah's life. That isn't much, but it was enough for them to ask him to preach at the subsequent funeral at their Pentecostal Church. We might consider such an invitation as a positive piece of an evidence-based outcome, but one cannot build much on such a thin reed. No one from the family's church, where they were said to be active, appears in any of the data. The family was seemingly bereft of attention and support, and the chaplain made himself available. However, it is difficult to assess how well the chaplain functioned or exactly what he meant to the family.

The parents were burdened with a three-year-old at home, the heavy demands of the husband's job, and their apparent idealism about the prospects for Sarah. There was no evidence cited of any social network of support for this struggling couple during the six-month hospitalization of their daughter. Perhaps the chaplain, thin reed that he was, represented the full extent of the family's caring resources.

In the written conclusion to the case, the chaplain claimed that he facilitated the infant Sarah's experience of the holy by introducing her to the rituals of her family's faith tradition. But can anyone think that an outcome for Sarah was her experience of the holy? The chaplain claimed so. But he would be laughed out of any clinically-based examination that attempted to demonstrate that claim in any way.

The claim that the chaplain introduced the infant Sarah to the Pentecostal rituals of the family's faith tradition seems equally implausible. I do not read that the chaplain was Pentecostal, and even if he were, I doubt an undeveloped six-month-old infant would absorb such rituals.

Thus there are no evidence-base outcomes in the case of Sarah, with possibly one exception. The family invited the chaplain to speak at Sarah's funeral in her home church. No one can build too much on that, but it does indicate a positive bond between family and chaplain, and while this is not much, it is something.

CASE 3

In the case of Vicki, a male-to-female transgender veteran, we can presume that the one-session meeting with the female chaplain therapist at the VA hospital, who was herself active in the LGBT community, was of some comfort. The chaplain assessed the veteran as having felt blessed by the consultation. While a tad self-serving, that assessment may well have been an accurate reading of the consultation. But aside from the chaplain's reporting, what is the evidence? How would anyone weigh the evidence and measure the supposed outcome? Is it quite enough to observe, from the chaplain's account, that the supplicant went away happy, or seemingly comforted? In our reading, this does not qualify as substantive evidence. And we also know that short-term outcomes sometimes get quickly reversed and can be seen as a kind of facade. If there was an evidence-based outcome from this case, it was not elaborated upon in the clinical write-up.

CASE 4

In the case of Mrs. Helen, who was obsessed for four decades over a priest whom she alleged had fondled her breasts while she slept next to him on a bus during a military excursion, we cannot see any substantive outcome whatsoever. There does not seem to have been any resolution of her complex sexual problem. So there is no real outcome to authenticate. But even if she had had serious psychotherapy and had come to an awareness of her profound conflicts over sexual pleasure, we would have to have her full cooperation to reach any final agreement that the outcome was significant and positive. A verifiable positive outcome in Mrs. Helen's case would require an in-depth interview with Mrs. Helen herself. To research the outcomes in Mrs. Helen's case would be a monumental and very personal task. For this, she would have to, in effect, relive the therapy, which of course, at this point, she has not experienced. As for evidence-based outcomes, Mrs. Helen seems to be where she was at the very beginning of her very long treatment, obsessed with priests and obsessed with sex. That amounts to no outcome at all. Chaplain Sanders claims that a significant evidence-based outcome was that Mrs. Helen was able to articulate her anger at the priest. I fail to see how expressions of anger are, by definition, therapeutic outcomes.

CASE 5

In the case of ten-year-old Paul, the pediatric and psychiatric patient, it is claimed by the chaplain that Carol, the mother, was able to express her honest feelings about being abandoned by God. That certainly is a positive outcome, however modest. The chaplain also claims that her prayer was a tangibly powerful experience for Carol. Possibly so, but I fail to see how that could be measured. At the same time, one has to wonder what the staying power is with such a prayer. And I do not know how that could be proven or even measured. The chaplain also contends that the rituals she offered proved to be precisely what the family needed, and that they softened the suffering. How is that measured? The chaplain's word on these matters hardly qualifies as an evidence-based outcome. It qualifies rather as a highly speculative, even fanciful, conjecture.

CASE 6

The measurable outcomes in the Asgeirsdottir case were stated as "a growing inner strength, security and some structure around the family's life" during this death. The chaplain contends that the rituals offered to the family were just what it needed, and softened their anguish and despair. It is claimed that this was achieved primarily through rituals and, as well, the chaplain's functioning as a family spokesperson.

That is a claim for specific outcomes, but it does not provide evidence. The evidence even appears somewhat to the contrary. At the burial service, the family erupted in anger at the selection of the burial site. How do we assess that? Since the eruption had a reactive quality, it would seem to be possible evidence of displaced, pent-up frustration. If the family had felt secure in the structure of the grieving process, as is claimed, why would they need to erupt? Had they been comfortable, they might have coolly registered their objection to the burial site and requested another. The evidence, in this case, suggests that the family was on edge, and hardly "growing in inner strength and security," as is claimed.

Thus the outcomes, in this case, are unclear, possibly even negative.

We all tend to see things as we wish they were.

CASE 7

Daisy, a colleague, and co-worker of the chaplain found herself with terminal-stage cancer. The chaplain in this case, being recently employed, had not known Daisy very well before her falling ill with a terminal condition. Gradually and tentatively, the chaplain befriended Daisy and ultimately saw her through her dying process. She did not brush Daisy off. But ultimately, the chaplain seemed to become Daisy's principal guide during her dying process and presided, at Daisy's request, over her funeral. We do not have access to the soul or inner thoughts of Daisy, but all the available data suggests that the chaplain served Daisy very well. Though this is indeed an outcome and an entirely positive one, it is not clear how solid the evidence is, and how it might be a measurable one. I would rather say that the evidence was impressionistic at best.

To play the devil's advocate here, suppose it happened that Daisy was simply tolerating the chaplain as the best of several bad options available to her, and hardly what she wished? Let us suppose Daisy had decided to simply make her peace with what was available in the dying process? Daisy is now dead and cannot talk. We have only the chaplain's view of the relationship. So who can tell now whether the chaplain was effective, or whether she was being put up with by the patient who saw no other options? That scenario would not be my best read on the relationship. However, most of the soft evidence of clinical pastoral work is based on best guesses, not measurable data.

There are other aspects of this case that are indeed more accessible to measurement. As a result of the chaplain's seemingly successful relationship with the dying Daisy, the newly employed chaplain is said to have gained a great deal of respect and goodwill from the hospital staff as a whole. That is something that could well be measured. A survey could have been conducted to report the chaplain's credibility before and after her ministry to Daisy, not that anyone would likely want to run such a survey, but it could be done.

Certainly, the chaplain was dedicated to Daisy and seemed to serve her well in her dying process over many months. The outcome of her work would appear to have been quite positive. But was it a measurable outcome? I don't fathom how it could be measured.

CASE 8

Here we have Mrs. Pearlman, an eighty-two-year-old woman with a terminal diagnosis of advanced Alzheimer's disease and severe mental confusion. The two anonymous chaplains assert that the patient was deeply engaged with them and "extremely emotionally expressive." They seem to posit that an emotionally labile state is a successful evidence-based outcome.

They also point out that the patient appears grateful. To be sure, she is treated with kindness and respect by the rabbi who presents the case. However, the garbled communication between the patient and anyone relating to her, including her rabbi, leaves unresolved the question of the actual outcome, as well as the evidence.

CASE 9

Steve Nolan, in his extensive pastoral work with the terminal patient, Kristof, acknowledged that the outcomes of his work were somewhat unclear and certainly not documentable. Nolan's work suggests a significant therapeutic relationship. But "suggests" is the determinative word here. The two psychiatrists who comment on his case are quite affirming, but they also hedge their definite conclusions with caveats, as well they should. Psychiatrists, as well as pastoral workers, are destined to perform services for others that can hardly ever be finally labeled successful in a way that is supported by evidence demonstrating effective outcomes. But we work on anyway, knowing in our bones that on balance the work we do is useful, even essential. Nolan's work with the dying Kristof leads me to the conclusion that it was, in spite of some errors, the kind of pastoral work that the whole world begs for.

SUMMARY

This small monograph does not further Fitchett's ambition to promote evidence-based outcomes in clinical pastoral work. For all his assertions, the evidence-based outcomes are nowhere to be found.

Evidence-based outcomes are simply difficult, even impossible, to isolate in the work of pastoral care, counseling, psychotherapy, and psychoanalysis. The interpersonal and intrapsychic nature of the pastoral relationship make it impervious to scientific scrutiny, examination, and assessment. The best we can come up with are informed guesses, perhaps good guesses, but guesses that are hardly or rarely ever evidence-based. Pastoral care, counseling, psychotherapy, and psychoanalysis are not exact sciences, if indeed they can be labeled science at all.

But Fitchett has an even more problematic burden in his call for evidence-based documentation of spiritual care. Unlike pastoral care, spiritual care is itself undefined. Even his co-editor Steve Nolan acknowledges that. As Nolan writes, "The lack of an agreed and articulated definition for spiritual care means that, as a profession, chaplains struggle to explain clearly the nature of the work." Fitchett has built his paean to evidence-based outcomes in spiritual care on quicksand.

When a pastor sits with a grieving family while they pour out their feelings, their memories, and their sorrows, what is the outcome? We know, of course, that there is healing in being able to vent one's feelings to someone who is listening and processing, even if the listener ultimately says nothing. We also know that gathering evidence of success in such cases is difficult to impossible.

In my first seminary course on pastoral counseling in 1961, Dr. William Oglesby played a wire recording of a counseling session he had conducted. A woman spoke of some terrible ordeal she had experienced, and Oglesby said only "Uh-huh" repeatedly for fifty minutes. Oglesby made his point. The voice of the suffering person and the silence of the sympathetic listener is central to healing, and sometimes all that is needed. That certainly does not mean that the pastoral counselor never speaks, but it does suggest that vocalizing one's pain to another is a large part of the therapy, sometimes even all of it.

In the instance of an appendicitis attack, surgery can remove the inflamed organ. Blood tests can be made to confirm infection. Post-surgery examination can confirm that the infection has been halted. Lab tests can confirm the disease of the organ that was excised. The outcome is clear and demonstrated by the laboratory. With that, we have evidence of success.

When physicians more than a century ago were stymied over Elizabeth von R's leg paralysis, she was referred to Freud, who listened to her story. She eventually left Freud's analysis and was soon able to dance. The outcome was thus clear. But where is the evidence that linked Freud to the cure? Freud and Elizabeth only talked, or rather Elizabeth talked, and Freud said very little. We now think we know that Elizabeth was cured when her shame over her fantasies of marrying her dead sister's husband, with whom she often took afternoon walks, was revealed and addressed. In divulging all this to Freud, she felt implicitly forgiven. We have to think that the outcome of Elizabeth's consultation with Freud was redemptive and healing. But we cannot take that cure to the lab for tests. The evidence is soft and cannot be articulated.

So in pastoral work, we sometimes see strong outcomes, but we are not usually able to link with certainty the treatment to the outcome. There are typically too many immeasurable variables. As with Freud, the evidence of a link between treatment and cure is slight and short-lived. That does not give the pastor a warrant to attribute healing to just any kind of listening. It is both more subtle and more complicated than that.

In fairness to Fitchett, we do not find him assuming the mechanical procedures of George Benson. But neither do we find the evidence-based outcomes that Fitchett touts. In the nine cases that Fitchett and Nolan have selected for this monograph, we find no procedures for discovering evidence-based outcomes. Worse than that, we see very little in the way of verifiable outcomes in any of the nine cases. We do not see outcomes even close to the subtle but dramatic outcome of Freud's work with Elizabeth von R.

THE ULTIMATE EVIDENCE-BASED OUTCOMES RESEARCH PROJECT

Dr. George Fitchett should have learned something already from Dr. George Benson's costly attempt to demonstrate the evidence of the beneficial effects of intercessory prayer. Both Benson and Fitchett seem eager to prove that pastoral (or spiritual, as they call it) work produces concrete results. But Benson believes results can be achieved by anonymous prayer, or something on the order of telepathy. Fitchett more wisely seems to believe that results come through personal contact and face-to-face prayer.

Early in the previous decade, George Benson, a Harvard professor with an M.D., launched a $2.4 million research project called the "Study of the Therapeutic Effects of Intercessory Prayer" (STEP), which was completed in 2006. STEP was also referred to as the "Templeton Foundation Prayer Study," citing the foundation that provided the funding. It was also known as the "Great Prayer Experiment." The research sought evidence-based results from intercessory prayer. The study enlisted 1,802 coronary patients in six hospitals, using double-blind protocols. It recruited a great many devout people from three Christian congregations to do the praying. None of those praying knew the people they were praying for. They were given only the first names and initials of surnames. The patients who were the recipients of the prayers were organized into three groups: Groups 1 and 2 were told that they might or might not be prayed for. In actuality Group 1 was prayed for; Group 2 was not. Group 3 was told that they would be prayed for, and they were. The three Christian congregations were enlisted to do so.

The delicious results of this study revealed that those who were not prayed for did marginally better health-wise than those in the other two groups who were in fact prayed for. The differences were not, of course, significant. The precise results of the study suggested that all the praying was of no consequence one way or the other, with the slight possibility that the prayers were actually harmful to health!

So much for the Great American Prayer Study!

It appears that Benson and his team never contemplated the dire consequences of success. If Benson could have demonstrated that vast numbers of people lobbying God through prayer could produce scientifically documented results, one can only imagine where that would leave the human species. God would be running an office for lobbyists to send in their requests for specific action in the world.

Such is the difficulty when one seeks hard evidence of therapeutic results from pastoral work. Had Benson's praying people visited the patients personally, and actually spent time listening to them, the results may well have been more salutary. The presence of a human being, in the flesh, even if untrained, might indeed have some therapeutic effect. However, in such a case, the therapeutic results could then have been attributed to personal contact rather than the workings of a *deus ex machina*.

It is quite likely that personal contact is an essential ingredient for prayer that can be demonstrated to be effective. But perhaps the personal contact is the source of healing, not the prayer. In that case, there must be an attempt at separating the effects of interpersonal contact and the prayer itself. It is likely that any positive results have to do simply with the personal contact itself and that the gods have no part in the process. If that were so, a personal visit without prayer might be potentially just as effective as one with prayer, or perhaps even more so.

ABOUT THE AUTHOR

Raymond J. Lawrence is a Virginian by birth who began his working life at age eight as a newspaper boy, then as a batboy for a professional baseball team, the Portsmouth Cubs. While in seminary he was ordained a Methodist minister and served rural churches in Chesterfield County, Virginia. Subsequently, he joined the Episcopal Church, was ordained a priest, and served congregations in Newport News, Virginia, and Knoxville, Tennessee. He holds an M.Div. from Presbyterian Theological Seminary in Richmond, an S.T.M. from the School of Theology, University of the South, and a D. Min. from New York Theological Seminary. He did two years of postgraduate studies at the University of St. Andrews in Scotland and at Mansfield College, Oxford University, in England. He completed two years of clinical training in residencies at St. Luke's Episcopal-Texas Children's Hospital in Houston and at Central State Hospital in Milledgeville, Georgia.

His life's work has been principally in the field of clinical pastoral care, counseling and pastoral psychotherapy. He was certified a clinical supervisor by the Association for Clinical Pastoral Education in 1970, and has held leadership positions within that organization. In 1988 he began publishing the *ACPE Underground Report,* which later became *Contra Mundum.* In 1990, with colleagues, he founded the College of Pastoral Supervision and Psychotherapy (CPSP) and has served as its General Secretary ever since. CPSP has grown from fifteen members in 1990 to approximately one thousand today. His last working position was as Director of Pastoral Care, New York Presbyterian Hospital, Columbia-Presbyterian Medical Center in New York City, a position he held for fifteen years.

Lawrence has published widely in the fields of social ethics, pastoral psychotherapy, sexuality, and religion. His articles have appeared in *The Journal of the American Medical Association,* the *Annals of Behavioral Medicine,* the *Journal of Religion and Health,* the *Journal of Pastoral Care and Counseling, The Christian Century, Christianity and Crisis,* and others. His opinions have appeared in *The New York Times, The Washington Post,* the *Los Angeles Times,* and a number of other newspapers. He has written five previous books: *The Poisoning of Eros: Sexual Values in Conflict,* (Augustine Moore Press, 1989), *Sexual Liberation: The Scandal of Christendom* (Praeger Press, 2007), *Nine Clinical Cases: The Soul of Pastoral Care and Counseling* (2015), *Recovery of Soul: A History and Memoir of the Clinical Pastoral Movement* (CPSP Press, 2017), and *Bursting the Bubble: The Tortured Life of David Vetter* (Augustine Moore Press, 2019). He is an amateur mycologist and founder of the Texas Mycological Society.

He is currently Dean of The Graduate Institute of the College of Pastoral Supervision and Psychotherapy.

He may be reached at lawrence@cpsp.org.